T0010625

A Treatise on Perfection

A Treatise
on
Perfection

Saintly Counsel on Obtaining Salvation

Cardinal Armand Jean du Plessis,
Duke of Richelieu

Translated by
Fr. Robert Nixon, OSB

TAN Books
Gastonia, North Carolina

English translation © 2023 TAN Books

All rights reserved. With the exception of short excerpts used in critical review, no part of this work may be reproduced, transmitted, or stored in any form whatsoever, without the prior written permission of the publisher. Creation, exploitation and distribution of any unauthorized editions of this work, in any format in existence now or in the future—including but not limited to text, audio, and video—is prohibited without the prior written permission of the publisher.

Cover design by Caroline Green

Cover image: Cardinal Richelieu on the sea wall at La Rochelle, 1881 (oil on canvas), (detail of 153763), Motte, Henri Paul (1846-1922) Bridgeman Images.

ISBN: 978-1-5051-2127-8
Kindle ISBN: 978-1-5051-2128-5
ePUB ISBN: 978-1-5051-2129-2

Published in the United States by
TAN Books
PO Box 269
Gastonia, NC 28053
www.TANBooks.com

Printed in India

"I entreated, and the spirit of Wisdom came to me.
And I valued her more highly than scepters and thrones.
Compared to her, I considered riches to be as nothing
and no priceless jewel to be her equal. . . .
Yes, I loved her more than the light itself!"
—Wisdom 7:7–10

Contents

Translator's Introduction

The name of Cardinal Richelieu will perhaps call to mind for most people the somewhat Machiavellian character in Alexander Dumas's beloved novel *The Three Musketeers*, or one of the various cinematic adaptations of that literary masterpiece. Alternatively, students of secular history may think of the skillful politician and accomplished statesman who exercised a guiding and even dominant influence over the political affairs of France, and indeed all of Europe, during the early seventeenth century. Yet the real Cardinal Richelieu (or more correctly and completely, Cardinal Armand Jean du Plessis, Duke of Richelieu) was, despite the multifaceted and complex nature of the work and activities in which he was involved, first and foremost a devout man of God, a dedicated priest, and an erudite scholar. It is true that prevailing circumstances compelled him to apply his abundant talents, wisdom, and industry to affairs of state and diplomacy rather than purely to the service of the Church. Yet this was the result of the inescapable necessities and the pressing needs of the time. As a politician, Richelieu was motivated by a genuine dedication to the common good and the flourishing of a genuinely Catholic state, more so than any other personal ambition or agenda.

Richelieu's Early Years

Armand Jean du Plessis, Duke of Richelieu, was born in 1585 to an ancient and noble family as the youngest son in a family consisting of three sons and two daughters. In terms of wealth and status, his hereditary estate was of a mediocre and even somewhat lowly order amongst the nobility of France. At that time, Richelieu itself was merely a tiny and virtually unknown rural hamlet in central France. However, the house of Richelieu did have within its sphere of influence the bishopric of Luçon and enjoyed, by royal privilege, the right to nominate to the monarch a candidate to occupy that episcopal seat. The king would, in turn, propose this nominee to the pope. For all practical purposes, however, this meant that the Richelieu family could effectively choose the person to serve as bishop of Luçon.

It was the original intention of the family that one of Armand's brothers, Alphonse, the second eldest son, should serve as bishop, while the eldest son would assume control of the patrimonial estate. However, when Alphonse (who is recorded as a man of the most distinguished sanctity and learning) renounced the world to become a Carthusian monk, the responsibility fell upon Armand by default. Until then, he had intended to pursue a career as an army officer— or, more accurately, his family had determined that it was fitting for him to pursue a military career, and he had acquiesced to their determination. Now, they determined that he would serve the Church.

Ascension to the
Episcopate and Political Power

It is clear that young Armand turned to his theological studies with real fervor and talent, perhaps sensing in them a field more suited to his vocation, propensities, and inclination than military life. An industrious and gifted student, he had obtained his doctorate with the highest possible distinction by the age of twenty. Indeed, while still a child, he had already displayed a precocious aptitude for the Latin language and philosophy. These skills he readily and fruitfully applied to the mastery of Sacred Scripture, theology, and canon and civil law, as well as the writings of the Church Fathers. At the age of twenty-two, he was ordained as bishop of Luçon by Pope Paul V. According to some sources, the pontiff was persuaded to ordain him before the canonically required minimum age (then twenty-three) on account of the impressive scope and depth of his learning, as well as his wondrous oratorical fluency in the Latin language.

Richelieu distinguished himself in the episcopal office by the effectiveness of his preaching, the competence of his administration, and his indefatigable zeal in his pastoral duties. When he assumed the bishopric, the Diocese of Luçon was in a dire state of deterioration, disorder, and decay due to a history of poor governance and both political and doctrinal uncertainty. Richelieu achieved a radical revitalization of the diocese, including the restoration of clerical discipline, the establishment of a seminary, the restoration of the cathedral and parish churches, and the nourishing of the faith life of both the laity and clergy through an extensive program of catechesis and pastoral visitations.

In 1614, he was selected to attend the Estates-General (a kind of parliament or consultative assembly by which the nobility, clergy, and commoners could advise and petition the king) as the representative of the clergy in the Poitou region. At this assembly, he displayed such eloquence, wisdom, and intelligence that he was immediately appointed to the service of the palace, who recognized the immense potential value of the talents of such a gifted youngster to the Crown.

Richelieu steadily rose to greater prominence and responsibility in the court. In 1622, he was raised to the dignity of
cardinal, and he became prime minister of France in 1624. For
the next eighteen years, he continued in this role—in effect, the
most powerful man in France—until struck with a grave illness
(possibly tuberculosis) in his fifty-seventh year. As his condition
worsened, churches throughout the nation held prayer vigils
before the Blessed Sacrament for the recovery of their beloved
protector and patron. Despite the fervent intercession of such a
multitude, Richelieu died in 1642. On his deathbed, he is said to
have repeated incessantly the words of the psalm, "*In manus tuas,
Domine, commendo spiritum meum,*"[1] as he returned his immortal
soul to his Creator and his body slept the sleep of earthly death.

RICHELIEU'S LEGACY, POLITICAL AND ECCLESIASTICAL

Despite the complexity and instability of the political conditions
at the time of Richelieu's ascendency, he was universally admired
for his competence, wisdom, and astuteness. When Peter the
Great, czar of Russia, visited the monument to the illustrious
cardinal in Paris, he is reported to have exclaimed, "O great man!
I would give to you half of my kingdom, to learn from you how
to govern the other half."

In evaluating Richelieu's character, there are many conflicting and even contradictory portraits available. These are, of
course, very often tinted by the particular perspectives of their
writers. The picture painted by Dumas is, of course, purely
fictional. It is historical fiction indeed, but it is historical only
insofar as the names, dates, and pivotal events are taken from

---

[1] "Into your hands, O Lord, I commend my spirit" (Ps 30:6).

history. Dumas depicts Richelieu as a bitter rival to the king, Louis XIII, for political and military supremacy in France. The great novelist even portrays Richelieu as being secretly motivated, at least in part, by an amorous infatuation with the wife of Louis XIII, Queen Anne of Austria. But such details, convincing and plausible as they are in the context of the novel, must be attributed entirely to the invention of Dumas's fertile imagination.

The actual evidence, if viewed objectively, suggests that Richelieu was instrumental in helping maintain the stability not only of France but of all Western Europe during what was an egregiously turbulent and complex era. He sought above all for peace and reconciliation between conflicting parties (or at least the refraining from violent conflict and the curtailing of needless bloodshed), both in matters of religion and secular governance.

But Didn't He Ally with the Protestants?

In his foreign policy as a political leader, Richelieu did not shrink from forming alliances with Protestant states against Catholic ones when this suited the interests of France and the broader interests of the stability of Europe and the Church (as he saw it). In the Thirty Years' War, Richelieu allied France with Protestant princes and the Swedish Protestant king against the Catholic Holy Roman Empire in order to secure advantages for France over its traditional rival, the Holy Roman Empire in Germany, which had dynastic connections to Spain—also a rival to France—and through Spain to the Netherlands.

Cardinal Richelieu is often faulted by Catholics for this for the obvious reason that he appeared to prefer to fight another Catholic power rather than ally with it in a common front against the Protestants; the argument is that he placed the particular interests of France over the universal need of the whole Catholic people. However, in Richelieu's own view, the empire was too weak or incapable of efficaciously defending Catholic interests. He believed that a strong France would best ensure the safety of Catholicism. In other words, Richelieu deemed that what was good for France was necessarily good for the Church in general.

In this context, it is important to note that France was traditionally identified as the "eldest daughter of the Church," and the French Crown was understood to be an inherently Catholic institution. Moreover, the Holy Roman Empire, despite also being Catholic, did not enjoy a uniformly harmonious relationship with the papacy, and the division of authority between the emperor and the pope had been a source of bitter contention throughout much of history. These considerations do not necessarily justify Richelieu's concrete choices in the Thirty Years' War, but they do show that he was not merely the unsavory or unscrupulous politician which Dumas made him out to be. Dumas made a caricature of a complicated man in a complicated time. It would be a small mind indeed that failed to see that these were prudential decisions in the political sphere and that they do not affect his orthodoxy, nor his piety and religion, in any way.

As an ecclesiastical leader, the cardinal played a key role in implementing the decrees of the Council of Trent in France. The fact that Pope Urban VIII, the great reforming pope of the seventeenth century, counted Richelieu among his closest personal friends and most highly esteemed colleagues and confidantes is a powerful testimony to the qualities and merits which he possessed as a man imbued with knowledge of the Catholic Faith.

CARDINAL RICHELIEU, ACCOMPLISHED SPIRITUAL AUTHOR

Richelieu's literary output included several significant and interesting works that display well his talented intellectual faculties dedicated to serving the Church. By far, the most influential during his lifetime was his *Instruction du chrestien* (also published in Latin as *Institutio Christiana*), a kind of catechetical manual or digest of the Catholic Faith. This book, written while he was serving as bishop of Luçon (which is to say, while he was in his twenties), achieved enormous popularity in its time. Originally written as instructional material for the people of his own diocese, it was soon officially adopted by the other bishops of France and gained a very wide circulation. Many diocesan bishops ordered passages from the book to be read in their cathedrals and parish churches on Sundays as a means of instructing, encouraging, and correcting the faithful. According to a contemporary commentator, its popularity was such that there was virtually no one in France who was not intimately acquainted with the book, and it had been translated into a multitude of foreign languages, including even Arabic and Turkish. This claim, though *prima facie* somewhat farfetched, is, in fact, borne out by published copies of such translations still in existence.

Another noteworthy and highly innovative work is his *Traitté qui contient la methode la plus facile et la plus asseurée pour conuertir ceux qui se sont separez de l'Eglise* (Treatise which contains an easy and certain method of converting those who are separated from the Church). Imitating Saint Francis de Sales's apologetical masterpiece, *The Catholic Controversy*, Richelieu's is a remarkable work of Catholic apologetics in which the soundness and solidity of the doctrines of the Church are capably expounded and clarified, and misconceptions and misrepresentations of the Catholic position are studiously and systematically dispelled. Avoiding a polemical or confrontational approach, it is uniformly courteous, mild, and reasonable in tone, anticipating many of the recommendations for ecumenical dialogue made by the Second Vatican Council. A notable example of this is Richelieu's preference for referring to Protestants as "those separated from the Church" rather than as heretics or schismatics.

In addition, there were many publications of Richelieu's private memoirs, his correspondence, and his state and diplomatic papers, all of which offer invaluable sources of historical data and insights into the political machinations of Europe in the seventeenth century. Of historical interest to the scholar are the several volumes falsely attributed to him (presumably for the sake of promoting sales), especially those released by English publishers. A fascinating and typical example is *On the Art of Pleasing in Conversation, Written by the Famous Cardinal Richelieu* of 1708, in which the cardinal is used as a fictitious personification of a witty, experienced, urbane, and somewhat calculating man of the world imparting advice to an ambitious youth on how to make a favorable impression in society. Richelieu is also reported to have written dramas and comedies for his own amusement and recreation, but these were never published and apparently do not survive.

Undoubtedly, however, the cardinal's masterpiece as an author is his extended treatise on Christian spirituality and virtue entitled *Traitté de la perfection du chrestien* in its French version of 1646 and *Tractatus de Perfectione Christiani* in the Latin version of 1651.[2] It is

---

[2]   In the introductory epistle to the Blessed Virgin Mary, Richelieu states that he commenced writing the book at the time when the Kingdom of France was officially dedicated to Our Lady. This was done, at his prompting, in 1638, some four years before his death.

this illuminating and valuable work which is offered here in English for the first time with the title *A Treatise on Perfection*.[3]

A TREATISE ON PERFECTION: HOW TO RULE ONESELF WELL

The present translation has been prepared principally from the original edition of the Latin text, with occasional references also to the French version where this has seemed helpful for the clarification of some nuance of meaning or tone. While it is, as far as the English idiom permits, a literal and direct translation, certain abridgments have been made at points when they have seemed judicious or advisable. These abridgments include the omission of the lengthy and rather scholastic discourses on the different varieties and classifications of mental prayer, and other similar topics in that vein. Since passages of this type are largely repeating or clarifying traditional terms and definitions, their omission takes little away from the original and particular substance of the book, while adding considerably to its readability and cohesiveness.

The book belongs to the genre of spiritual guidebooks intended primarily for laypersons. Such guidebooks enjoyed considerable popularity in the century following the Council of Trent, especially among Francophone readers. They responded to the pastoral needs of an emerging class of educated and reflective people who, while not called to consecrated religious life, sincerely sought to advance in Christian spirituality and virtue. For modern readers, the best-known example of a work of this type is certainly *The Introduction to the Devout Life* by Saint Francis de Sales, whom Richelieu admired and venerated deeply, and from

---

[3]   A more strictly literal (if unidiomatic) translation of the title would be *Treatise on the Perfection of the Christian*.

whom he quotes at certain points. But there were innumerable other publications of treatises from that era of this type, covering topics such as the practice of prayer and meditation, the cultivation of virtue, and the balancing of a spiritual life with the practical responsibilities of one's state in the world.

The spiritual approach outlined by Richelieu is one which evidently draws very much upon his own experiences—namely, those of a person who aspired to lead a meritorious and spiritually fruitful life, yet who was immersed in a world which presented numerous and varied challenges to this aspiration. Foremost amongst these challenges were the complex and onerous demands of his work as a public servant, statesman, and political advisor. Such work—then as now—is seldom free of ambiguous and ambivalent ethical questions. And while portrayals of the French court in the seventeenth century in literature and cinema may often be inclined to exaggerate its corruption, intrigues, and moral laxity, there can be little doubt that these were all realities which Richelieu frequently encountered. Moreover, the circles in which he lived and worked were ones in which material luxury prevailed conspicuously and was taken for granted. Even though such luxury did not accord at all with his own personal inclinations, he could scarcely hope to escape it entirely while carrying out his duties effectively. These duties involved the cultivation of easy social relationships with persons of high status, and for this reason, his manners and mode of life had to be broadly congruent with theirs.

But despite the opulence, extravagance, and moral ambiguities of the world in which he lived, the cardinal strove always to maintain true integrity of soul and genuine simplicity of heart. His approach to spirituality is a very pragmatic and practical one. According to this approach, it is best to adopt a style and form of prayer which is moderate, sustainable, and suited to one's state of life rather than attempting one which is perhaps more elevated and demanding but entirely unsustainable in the long term. His aptitude for being a successful political ruler and wisdom gained thereby shows itself in his treatment on how to rule oneself well. Judging the particular circumstances of one's life by the virtue of prudence is imperative. It is always wisest to make the best of circumstances as they actually are rather than dreaming of and aspiring to imaginary and impossible alternatives.

THE PRINCIPAL POINTS OF THIS WORK

Fulfill Your State in Life Well

Central to Richelieu's approach is the notion that fulfillment of one's proper and legitimate duties in the world is the single most important moral responsibility of the Christian, and also the most effective form of prayer. At the time at which he wrote, there was far less social mobility than there is today. A person's status in the world, profession, or role—even the selection of a marriage partner or the discernment of a religious vocation—was largely determined by external circumstances rather than by free or individual choice. Even then, Richelieu encourages the reader to accept the realities of life as one finds them, as being determined by the mysterious will of a benevolent and wise God. To give one's full attention to the fulfillment of one's responsibilities with charity and diligence was thus to act in accordance with the sacred dispositions of Divine Providence. And since—according to the current view—social and political regimes were established and legitimized by this same Divine Providence, all genuinely Christian acts would be consistent with the prevailing secular and social order, together with the multitude of obligations, restrictions, responsibilities, and duties it prescribes or expects.

This position has a sound scriptural and philosophical foundation, reflecting the teaching in the first letter of Peter: "For the sake of the Lord, accept the authority of every human institution."[4] Yet it is perhaps somewhat problematic for many Christians today since the sense of social, political, and economic structures as being divinely ordained realities is far less strong than it was previously. Few people today, for example, would accept the notion of a hereditary monarchy or aristocracy as a manifestation of God's will. Nevertheless, the notion that a person's legitimate and proper duties in the world—including duties to his family, the Church, his profession, his nation, or his community—are ultimately done in the service of God's plan remains a useful and valid one. For parents, the best prayer they can offer is to be good parents. For those engaged in a particular profession, to serve others well through that profession is their truest form of devotion to God.

Salvation Is Easy—for the Christian

Another striking suggestion made by Richelieu is that the path leading to eternal salvation is, in fact, an easy one—or at least, a relatively easy one. At first glance, this may strike many as contrary to conventional Christian wisdom—does not Our Lord say that "the way that leads to life is hard and narrow"?[5] Yet Richelieu does not maintain that the Christian life is *entirely* free from suffering or adversities, which is hardly possible for any human being in any circumstance. No human life is ever completely "easy." Rather, he suggests that a life of Christian virtue is, on the whole, much easier, happier, and more satisfactory than a life given over to sin or vice. Moreover, since a life lived in obedience

---

4   1 Peter 2:13.
5   Matthew 7:14.

to God's law accords best with our true human nature, it is necessarily easier and happier than one lived in any other manner. Compared to any other form of living, salvation is easiest to attain within practice of Christian virtue in the Catholic Faith.

In offering this view, it is evident that the cardinal is speaking from his own rich and varied treasury of observations of the human condition. A life of moral rectitude and virtue tends, in almost all cases, to be more peaceful, stable, and tranquil than a life of sin, crime, or debauchery. Richelieu cites, in particular, the example of sexual immorality, which he asserts never leads to any real happiness or satisfaction but ultimately only to disgust, tedium, and a truncation of personal freedom. Furthermore, sins and crimes of any kind are inevitably accompanied by some degree of anxiety, fear, and guilt. For this reason, the happiness, advantages, and even pleasures that sin may appear to promise soon prove to be mere illusions.

Eternity Must Be Our Chief Concern

Finally, despite (or perhaps, because of) Richelieu's broad and penetrating experience of worldly affairs, he proposes that it is the eternal destiny of the soul which should be a human being's chief concern. The things of this world are, at best, temporary and contingent. Compared to the eternal life of the immortal soul—both in respect to duration and quality—the joys and sorrows of this life amount to very little, but a passing moment, as it were. It therefore behooves each person to consider his eternal fate very seriously indeed, since it will constitute the final and permanent destination of his soul. Accordingly, all decisions in the present life should be made in the context of the eternity that awaits.

The cardinal writes extensively and even poetically on the joys of heaven in the second chapter of the treatise, which is perhaps the most beautiful and striking portion of the entire work. In the third chapter, he paints the terrors of damnation in equally vivid colors, summoning up a truly frightening vision of hell. Of course, few contemporary spiritual writers are inclined to introduce the fear of hell, at least as it is traditionally imagined, as a valid or effective motive for the cultivation of a virtuous life. Yet if Richelieu may seem somewhat dated in this respect, it is important to remember that the realities of both heaven and hell remain foundational elements of the Christian Faith and central pillars of its doctrines.

Since God is the true source and perfection of all happiness, to seek earnestly for eternal happiness in the life to come (as Richelieu so convincingly advises) and to love God are ultimately one and the same thing. Since happiness consists in the enjoyment of goodness, and God Himself is the epitome and source of all true goodness, to separate the pursuit of genuine personal happiness from devotion to God is, in fact, a false dichotomy.

RICHELIEU'S TEACHINGS TODAY

It is suggested that the spirituality of Richelieu, while imbued with the attitudes and realities of seventeenth-century France, offers much that is of value and relevance to the twenty-first--century Christian. Many contemporary Christians, like Richelieu, find themselves dealing with complex and demanding responsibilities and ethical questions which do not present any simple or univocal answers. For people in such situations, the present work offers sound and solid guidance by showing how the diligent fulfillment of secular responsibilities and duties can become a means of giving glory to God. One might say that Richelieu offers a spirituality of social duty—something sorely needed in our present age of apathy and alienation.

The fact that his approach is gently moderate and highly rational will strike a note of appeal for many modern readers. He speaks little of visions, revelations, and mystical experiences, and his manner of expression and arguments are all conspicuously reasonable, calm, and even dispassionate. He was a contemporary of René Descartes, and he exhibits something of the same desire to demonstrate the rational and intelligible character of the Christian doctrine and the consistency of Christian morality with both social and natural laws.

It is the hope of the present translator that many readers will find much to sympathize with in the person and thought of Richelieu—a man who was admittedly not quite a saint but certainly not a villain either. He indeed possessed all the wisdom of the serpent, though he fell, at times, rather short of the innocence of the dove. On a practical level, he was pragmatic, astute, and perhaps inclined to be unscrupulous when necessity or the common good seemed to demand it of him. Yet on a spiritual and religious level, he was deeply and unwaveringly loyal to the doctrines and hierarchy of the Church and animated with a most earnest desire for the eternal beatitude of heaven. Recalling Saint Teresa of Avila's famous advice that the primary quality in electing a spiritual director is to select a man learned in the spiritual life,[6] we would be hard-pressed to find a man more learned in the spiritual life and able to express it well than Cardinal Richelieu. And it was upon this, the spiritual life and its natural culmination in heaven, that his heart remained faithfully and lovingly fixed throughout his life. With some justice, Cardinal Richelieu might be characterized as being a wonderful, albeit imperfect, example of one who sincerely endeavored always "to render unto Caesar the things which are of Caesar, and unto God the things which are of God."[7]

---

[6]   *Way of Perfection,* chapter 5.

[7]   Matthew 21:22.

Dedicatory Epistle

To the most holy Virgin, Mother of God.

O great and holy Virgin, there are many cogent reasons why I should dedicate to you this work, which deals with the attainment of Christian perfection. For it was your own Son who came into the world to teach us such perfection, both by His holy words and the wonderful example of His manner of life. And it was you yourself who, after your only-begotten and Divine Son, embraced and displayed most fully and perfectly all the aspects of Christian virtue and sanctity.

Furthermore, I commenced the writing of this present work at the same time when this entire Kingdom of France was most solemnly consecrated to you, O Virgin Queen, and commended to your glorious patronage.[8] It would therefore be utterly inexcusable on my part if, at such a time, I failed to dedicate to you also my own humble writings.

I should fear, however, that my efforts should prove entirely unworthy to offer to you unless I was confidently depending upon your kindly assistance to help me. Through this assistance, I hope to gain the blessing of your Divine Son for both myself,

---

[8]   In 1638, Louis XIII dedicated the Kingdom of France to the Blessed Virgin. This consecration of the kingdom appears to have been an initiative of Richelieu.

as the author, and for this little book I am writing. Indeed, since I offer both myself and this book to you, His glorious Mother, it is fitting that your divine Son should look kindly upon my endeavors and efforts.

It is truly impossible for any Christian to praise and honor your Son, who is Lord of all the universe, with due and fitting reverence. For this reason, we honor you, His most holy Mother. For in embracing you with love and reverence, we embrace Him also. And the surest way we can honor and glorify His most holy name is through your merciful grace and kindly assistance. For you and He both draw virtue and power from the same Divine font. And it is through His merits that I trust that you will give generous assistance to me and be lovingly present to me as I work. And your Son's sacred wounds—the glorious price of our salvation—shall heal whatever deficiencies and shortcomings there are the prayers and vows I offer you.

Thus with my eyes fixed upon Christ as the head, I shall endeavor to teach the way which He established, exemplified, and taught. And though I may try to indicate this way to others, I cannot—alas!—claim to demonstrate it in my own life or person. It behooves each Christian to strive assiduously after this way of perfection. And, although this is something which I myself approach only in words and intentions, I pray that each person who truly seeks it may find it, and those who earnestly strive after it may attain it.

There is nothing you are not able to do, O Mary, through the immense love which God bears you! It was because of this infinite and glorious love that you received the incomparable dignity of being the Mother of the omnipotent and only God. And you desire above all else that this God, who is also your only-begotten Son, should be praised, glorified, and blessed forever and ever.

I pray therefore that, through your kindly and maternal aid, this work may prove useful and edifying—both to the souls of those for whom it is written as a guidebook and also to myself, its author, who invoke and implore your protection at each and every moment of my life, and most especially at the hour of my death.

I remain, my dearest Lady,
Your most devoted and ever-loving servant,
Richelieu

Author's Preface

———— •◆• ————

I must firstly acknowledge and defer, with all due humility, to the great merits and abilities of all the illustrious multitude who have already treated the theme which I am to consider in my present work. However, there are many such spiritual and moral treatises which are, despite their indisputable value and penetration, extremely lengthy and somewhat difficult to understand. For this reason, they are often not able to be absorbed by the reader without much laborious and even prohibitive effort. Therefore—motivated by charity, that kindly power which is able to accomplish all things—I myself shall compile and propose a method of achieving perfection in the Christian life, which is both short and easy.

Nonetheless, those who have devoted their efforts to this endeavor before me have certainly surpassed whatever my own humble attempts are or shall be, and have produced works which are more useful and which bear better and more substantial fruit than my own. They have already triumphantly run the course upon which I shall now tentatively dare to embark. But my intention in following their footsteps is not only to profit and instruct others but also to nourish and guide my own soul in its reflections and considerations.

If anyone who happens to read this modest work wishes to place their trust in what is contained herein, may they walk the path which I shall open to them with confidence, security, and alacrity. If I am able to promote or assist others in finding the way that leads to salvation by rendering such a service, I shall certainly have made some advances in arriving at my own.

The philosophers teach us that it is some final end or ultimate goal that motivates and determines each person or thing in their particular actions. Hence, we ought to consider carefully what our own final end or goal is, or what is the ultimate reward for which we are seeking. The way of Christian perfection has a two-fold objective: firstly, one that pertains to the individual's own benefit—namely, the attainment of personal salvation—and, secondly, one that pertains to God Himself—namely, that the divine glory may radiate forth ever more splendidly.

When these two things are considered, it will be realized that the first objective is finite in its nature and scope, whereas the second is without end. Hence, it is that when a person has progressed in virtue to the point where his own salvation is established, the pursuit of the second objective—that is, the glorification of God—still remains to compel him to yet further cultivation of the perfection of life, in imitation of the example of Christ Himself. It is impossible for persons genuinely committed to the glorification of God not to achieve their own personal salvation. It is similarly impossible for a person to arrive at true personal salvation without contributing, in some way, to the glorification of God. For this reason, the twin objectives of the Christian life—the attainment of individual salvation and the glorification of God—are always and inseparably bound together.

The nature of Christian perfection, which brings the human being both to individual salvation and to the glorification of God, is something which should be considered carefully and prudently. It will suffice for me to speak of it in general terms in order to manifest the way of virtue to which each is called, in accordance with the twofold objective of Christian perfection. Indeed, those who are at an earlier stage in the spiritual life will be motivated primarily by the desire for individual salvation, whereas those who are more perfect will seek primarily for the glory of God. This may perhaps be compared to the difference between infants who are scarcely able to run and still need to be nourished with milk and those who have reached maturity and can accept solid food. Similarly, those at the beginning of the Christian life need to be encouraged by considerations of personal rewards and punishments, but, little by little, they arrive at a state in which the glory of God becomes their sole motivating force, leading, in turn, to the ultimate crown of virtue.

In order that the perusal of this book may bear its best fruit, it behooves the readers to apply themselves attentively and to read without excessive haste so that there may be ample leisure for due reflection. Above all, the reader is advised always to strive to elevate his mind to God and to implore God's gracious assistance in achieving a sound understanding of what is written, together with a fruitful observance and practice of its recommendations.

Finally, there is a need for what has been read to be called back to mind from time to time for further meditation and reflection. This may be compared to the practice of certain ruminant animals that chew the food they have consumed repeatedly in order to extract from it purer sap and richer nourishment. The importance of the matters addressed herein demands, by its very nature, this careful diligence—since it is nothing less than eternity itself, and the cultivation of an effective and reliable method of arriving at the blessed state of everlasting happiness.

CHAPTER I

That Christians ought to give diligent care to their eternal salvation, in view of the great dignity of the human soul

———— ◆ ————

The pure light of natural reason clearly declares that God truly exists. This is apparent to all persons who are willing to employ such reason, and even to those of the most limited mental capacity. Faith, confirming this self-evident truth, similarly teaches those who are illuminated by its light that God must indeed exist. It affirms also that God, on account of the goodness and justice which are essential to His divine nature, shall return to each person eternal rewards or eternal punishments, according to what one has justly deserved while in this mortal life. For this world exists primarily as a stadium for merit and a period of testing. "I will come quickly!" says the Lord, "and I shall bring my rewards with me, to give to each person according to what their deeds deserve."[9]

Truly, those who ignore and disregard their own salvation are enveloped in a darker blindness than those who are born

---

[9]   Revelation 22:12.

completely without sight. Those who neglect to do such things that are necessary to their eternal happiness must certainly have hearts which are harder and more obdurate than stone!

The great dignity of the human soul may be perceived from its divine origin, from its deiform nature, from its celestial final destiny, and by the great price—namely, the precious blood of Christ—by which it was redeemed from everlasting perdition. These considerations should prevent us from lightly permitting our precious and immortal souls to be plunged into the abyss of eternal misery, either by our sins or by our foolish negligence. Rather, this realization of the soul's intrinsic dignity compels us to seek earnestly after the sublime heights of final blessedness by means of that divine grace which is the true and only seed of celestial glory.

Since God Himself is the Creator of our souls, they were each made bearing the image and "signature" of God. And they are therefore destined to return to God. This is expressed in the wonderful teachings of Saint Augustine, who asserts that since God is the Creator of human beings, the final objective and ultimate purpose of human beings is to partake in the being of God. Each human being carries within himself an image of his Creator— something which is spiritual, invisible, and immortal. Of course, as long as we live in this mortal life, our essence is circumscribed and confined by the limitations of time and space. But when our short earthly existence is ended, each soul is ultimately destined to pass into the infinite realm of eternity, in which all limitations and bounds are entirely transcended.

Just as the soul imparts life to the body, so it is that God imparts life to the soul. And, this being the case, is it possible for the soul to wish to separate itself from eternal life and divine beatitude? If we frown upon the act of murder, whereby a soul is separated from a body, should we not be more alarmed at those sins which separate the soul from God? As Saint Bernard says, does it make sense for anyone to pour out tears that a soul and a body are separated through physical death and not to pour our tears all the more abundantly when a soul is separated from God through sin?

And if God is the Creator of all things, including each human soul, is it not necessarily the case—as Saint Augustine expresses so eloquently—that the human soul will not find true rest except in God alone?

For whatever is set into motion is not able to rest until it arrives at the end of its particular course of motion. When a stone falls, it has no rest at the beginning of its fall. While it flies through the air, it similarly has no rest. But when it reaches the end of its course and settles on the earth, then it finally knows its place of rest. As for we human beings, the beginning of our journey is from the earth, then through the earthly realm. But our place of rest is in heaven. It is therefore in heaven alone that we shall delight entirely in God. Upon this earth, no true or complete tranquility is able to be found. As Saint Bernard says, there is no created thing that is capable of satisfying the longings of the soul. Created things are certainly able to distract or occupy the soul for a time, but they are never able to fulfill it. God alone is able to do this, since each soul is imbued with the capacity to receive God. Whatever is less than the glorious infinitude of God must therefore fail to satisfy the yearnings of the soul.

Is it possible for a soul, illuminated by the light of this realization, to disregard and ignore such things? Or is it possible for the soul—aware that it is destined for the eternal possession of the beatitude of God—to allow itself to be deprived of this infinite goodness so that it may seek instead the passing corruption of the world and the flesh?

Next, let us consider the precious blood of the Son of God. This was indeed paid as the price for the redemption of our souls. Are we then able to value our souls so cheaply that we disregard this most precious blood, this royal and divine ransom? Christ willed to suffer death in order to save our souls. Are we not bound then to value our own souls accordingly, since they have been redeemed at such a noble and incalculable price?

If, as Saint Gregory the Great observes, it is a happy thing when a mortal body is spared from physical death, is it not a much greater thing when an immortal soul is saved from eternal death? If we are not able to contemplate the physical death of one of our loved ones with dry eyes, should we be able to endure the eternal perdition of an immortal soul without much greater tribulation? Should we weep for those whose physical death no mortal could have prevented, and yet not weep more fervently over the damnation of souls, which, by simple penitence and contrition of heart, may have easily been saved?

Regarding the relationship of the mortal body and the immortal soul, Saint Augustine gives us the following dialogue. The souls says to the body, "I have descended from heaven to lead you from this mortal misery to divine perfection. Is it not better that you should follow me upwards to the heavens rather than that I should follow you downwards to the inferno?"

I may add something to these striking words. There is nothing, nothing at all, in this lower world which is not passing, deceptive, and conditional. Conversely, there is nothing in the upper world—the celestial realm of heaven—which is not eternal and perfect. This earth offers us anxiety, trial, and labor, whereas heaven is full of ineffable joy, infinite peace, and transcendental beatitude. Therefore, simple reason itself dictates that we should seek the infinite and eternal good things that are of heaven and renounce the ephemeral and limited things that are of the earth.

Furthermore, this means that each person should not only seek his own personal salvation but should also do whatever he reasonably can to promote the salvation of others. Indeed, this consideration was the motivating force which induced me to write the present work. But nevertheless, in finding and describing the way that leads to salvation, I must perforce instruct and guide myself first before I venture to advise any others. Indeed, to work for one's own salvation and that of others are so closely connected as to be practically inseparable. For if we devote our efforts to promoting the genuine well-being and eternal felicity of the souls of others, we shall thereby certainly achieve also the salvation of our own souls, as if by an infallible path. And similarly, if we diligently seek our own salvation, we cannot fail to guide and assist others as well.

We may recall from the pages of Sacred Scripture how Jonathan was sentenced to death by his father, King Saul, because he had placed a rod into a honeycomb and—contrary to the king's orders—tasted some of the honey. Yet he then went on to achieve an illustrious victory for the royal forces. This compelled his father the king to revoke the sentence against him, and thus Jonathan was freed.[10] Similarly, whatever crimes a sinner should carry with him before the tribunal of judgment of the Divinity, if such a sinner has procured so great a victory as bringing other souls to salvation, then these souls shall certainly implore mercy from God on behalf of that sinner. They shall cry out for leniency, just as the people of Israel did on behalf of Jonathan. And it is certain that God—whose sweetest delight is to pour forth good things to human beings—shall respond to such

---

[10]   1 Samuel 14:24–31, 43–45.

intercessions with clemency, allowing the hand of justice to be bound in the chains of love.

As Saint James writes, "Whoever converts a sinner from the error of his ways covers up a multitude of sins."[11] And we may place confidence in the words of Saint Dionysius the Areopagite, with which I shall conclude this chapter: "Among all the works of human beings, those that cooperate with God to bring about the salvation of other souls most perfectly imitate the nature of the Divinity. It is therefore such works that draw the soul closest to the beatitude of the Godhead."

---

[11] James 5:20.

Chapter II

On the brevity and anxiety of the present life, and the eternity and felicity of the life to come

———————— ◆ ————————

A fter a little reflection, we each must inevitably realize that this present life is really nothing but a pilgrimage. Compared to the vastness of eternity, it is but a moment in time. We must realize, furthermore, that it is a path filled with thorns and that we can barely take a step on it without experiencing some form of injury or pain. And we must similarly understand that the future life in heaven is, by its very nature, without end and extends into everlasting and boundless horizons of infinitude. In such a state, we will be free of all discomfort and affliction and shall rather enjoy forever the purest perfection of all good things. This being the case, how is it then that we should prefer the bad to the good, the limited to the infinite, and what is merely temporary anxiety to glorious eternity?

And, knowing and understanding these truths, it is impossible not to give special and primary care to the condition of one's immortal soul. But for anyone not to know these things seems scarcely possible, except for one willfully wrapped up in utter blindness by his own stubbornness and perverse desire to remain in darkness.

If we reflect upon the duration of our present earthly lives, we may profitably call to mind the words of Scripture that say, "My life is as a wind, and my days pass away like to the fleeting shadows."[12] And, in another place, "You do not know what will befall you tomorrow."[13] And again, "All flesh is like the grass of the field, and the glory thereof like the flower of the field. The grass withers, the flower fades."[14]

Blessed Augustine, in his magisterial exposition of the Psalms, observes that the days of human life are to be counted as being almost nothing, since before they were, they were nothing, and after they have passed, they will similarly be nothing. Even while our mortal lives are in existence, they are constantly in the process of passing away. Therefore, they never truly *exist* but are always merely in a state of becoming, or a transition from one nothingness to another nothingness. Indeed, this entire mortal life may be understood as a passage towards death, or a gradual process of dying.

And for all human beings, to cease to live—as the final and inescapable destiny of earthly life's journey—is the one unchangeable and indisputable reality of our condition, the one thing we all have in common. And we never know the moment when we shall cease to be. How much time one has left is known to no one, not even the wisest. And the time which has passed us by already is no longer our possession but is lost forever and irretrievably. Therefore, we may only properly call "life" the single instant of any given present, the infinitesimal point separating the phantasm of the future from the shadows of the past.

---

12   Psalm 143:4.
13   James 4:14.
14   Isaiah 40:6.

But this fleeting and fugacious present moment that constitutes the reality of life is itself a mere elusive "nothing"—in a perpetual state of flux and escape. It flees us even as we attempt to grasp it. With every instant, it is seized away from us to be consigned forever to the oblivion of nonexistence.

Although life and death seem to be contradictory and adversaries insofar as one excludes the other, they are so intrinsically connected that they travel together along the same path. Life and death may never be truly separated from each other in this sphere of existence. For until we arrive at the final moment of life, the possibility and anticipation of death must be our perpetual companion, as a shadow which is constantly cast over us, and as the sword of Damocles suspended above our heads.[15]

And although our life is extremely brief in comparison with the eternity which follows it, we so often abuse and waste even the limited period of time it affords us. Indeed, we often seem to strive with all our capacity to render it even shorter than nature or necessity has determined.

To live slothfully or lazily is hardly to live at all. And to live in a vicious or sinful manner may be described more accurately as death than life. If anyone were to be promised just one year to live and—according to usual human custom—spent much of his time in the pursuit of vices and sins, and wasted some of it in idle leisure and sloth, and then expended much of the remainder in fulfilling imagined social obligations, how little actual time would be left to him? A week? A day? An hour? Indeed, barely a

---

[15]   Damocles was, according to classical tradition, a courtier who was permitted to assume the position of king for a time. However, the condition of this was that while he was king, a sharp sword was to be suspended over his head by a fragile thread to emulate the constant anxiety and insecurity under which the real king lived. He soon chose to resign the role of king and return to his former life as a servant.

moment should remain! And there are many who live constantly in such manner, year after year, even for the entirety of their lives.

But they do not genuinely enjoy a *long* life, for they have let the time of their life slip away badly, uselessly, or wastefully. If we may speak in a philosophical manner, it is one thing truly to live and another thing merely to observe the passing by of one's days and years.

Then, if I look to the Sacred Scriptures, which are inspired by the very source of eternal truth itself, I read, "Human beings are born but to labor." "Their days are filled with thorns and pains, and even at night they are troubled."[16] "Heavy is the burden laid upon the shoulders of all the descendants of Adam, from the day they emerge from their mothers' wombs, until the day they return to the earth, the mother of us all."[17]

If after studying these divine oracles, I turn to the writings of the saints, I read that either bad things, or fear of bad things, is the constant companion of human beings during this troubled earthly sojourn. Our mortal existence is a time of ceaseless labor. We are conceived in darkness, then brought forth in pain. Once we are born, the first sounds we utter are those of desperate crying, accompanied by the ceaseless flow of tears.

I must indeed mourn the patent foolishness of those who expend infinite trouble, effort, and anxiety to acquire possessions and status which bring to them no real happiness and endure but for a passing moment. And yet the very same people will often neglect the acquisition of that true eternal salvation whose happiness and duration has neither end nor limit!

Virtually all of Sacred Scripture bears testimony to the superlative happiness and boundless eternity of the future life. Saint

---

[16]   Cf. Genesis 3:17–19; Job 7; 14:1; Psalm 89:10.

[17]   Sirach 40:1.

Paul speaks of it in such clear terms that there is no room for doubt or ambiguity when he writes, "Our present troubles are but slight and short-lived compared to the eternal glory which awaits us. The things which we now perceive are passing, but those things which are as yet unseen are eternal."[18]

As Saint Augustine notes, the life of the blessed would not be truly and completely blessed unless they were assured it was to last forever. For the one who possesses some good thing which may be lost is always haunted by the fear of losing it, and therefore does not enjoy perfect tranquility even in its possession. Saint Bernard declares that only eternal happiness would constitute the plenitude of happiness. The only happy end, writes he, is eternal life. And, paradoxically, the only happy ending is to find that happiness which has no ending.

But this heavenly beatitude transcends all limits and bounds, not those of duration only. The saints teach us that this blessedness is an aggregation of all possible goodness and of all possible joy. Thus, all the yearnings of the body and of the spirit are at once fulfilled to their utmost extent in the heavens. Not even the least possible object of desire shall be absent or lacking from this perfection.

For this reason, Saint Augustine, in describing the blessings of paradise, speaks of the fullness of light, peace, love, wisdom, glory, truth, sweetness, harmony, joy, and endless serenity. We may also speak of these blessings without difficulty and enumerate them glibly and easily; yet truly to conceive them, genuinely to imagine them as they really are—this is indeed quite beyond all our mortal capacities!

Although we may speak of it, we cannot possibly claim to know what it is to enjoy that perfect life in the heavenly homeland:

---

[18]   2 Corinthians 4:17.

perfect in well-being, in freedom from suffering, and in liberty, strength, and spiritual and intellectual perspicuity. There, we shall be robed in an ineffable splendor that will rival, or indeed surpass, that of the sun itself!

Our eyes shall be filled with the sight of a beauty which exceeds that of all human glory. We shall experience a delight like that of radiant lilies springing up in a shaded valley. We shall be illuminated by the incomparable luminance of a golden day that knows neither end nor close.

Indeed, there is no blessing or delight that we shall not then enjoy in that celestial realm where we shall dwell in a state utterly free from suffering, perfect in health and vigor, infused with absolute subtlety, energy, and agility, and robed in a glorious splendor like that of the stars themselves.

Each of our senses shall be saturated with the fullness of exquisite pleasure. Our eyes shall be seized and captured by the vision of beauty exceeding that of human imagination, emerging like the perfect rose of transcendent refulgence, sprung up from the midst of thorns. And this shall all be made splendid with the crystalline brilliance of an infinite day. Our ears shall be satiated with the sweetest harmonies of the celestial choirs, singing endless and inconceivable rhapsodies of praise to the supernal Godhead, in wave upon wave of heavenly song. Our nostrils shall be filled with the fragrances of paradise, the perfume of the divine beloved, the scent of myriads of myriads of star-born blossoms. Our sense of taste will be inebriated with the waters of the stream of all heavenly delights, and the golden nectar of nameless and indescribable pleasures. Our sense of touch will be utterly overcome with the warm embrace of an all-consuming love, transcending every human love and every fleshly sensation.

And there shall be nothing which the angels and saints possess that we also shall not possess in its entirety. There will be perfect peace without the slightest agitation, perfect rest without any labor, complete joy without the slightest stain or hint of sadness or regret—in short, all good things, unmixed with any tincture of evil or stain of sorrow.

The totality of this blessedness may be summarized as the vision of God, who is the essence and perfection of all goodness. In that future state, we shall perceive God face-to-face and no longer "through a glass and darkly"[19] as we do now. We shall behold the Divinity in essence and in nature, not only through its effects. This beatific vision shall be unmixed with the slightest trace of fear or trepidation. And although it will endure for all eternity, there shall never be a hint of tedium, satiety, or any suggestion of weariness or fatigue.

We shall enjoy this blessed eternity in a state of absolute freedom, which is at once both freely chosen by our own wills and desires and also completely and utterly necessary. It will be in accordance with our own will and desire because we shall continue to wish for this one divine objective forever. Yet it will also be completely necessary since the infinite perfection of God compels, as it were, all those who perceive it completely to the most profound and pure love thereof. We shall both behold and love God in an absolute, perfect, and complete manner. Verily, these two acts—that of beholding and that of loving—shall be truly one and the same.

For to perceive God in eternity is to be inflamed with the most ardent love for Him. To adhere to God totally, with all one's strength, will, and desire, constitutes the state of the most perfect happiness. And this is something beyond the limits of

---

[19]   1 Corinthians 13:12.

what any created being may experience in this deceptive, illusory, and transitory realm of time and space.

If anyone should enquire about what precisely is this glorious vision of God of which we speak, let him know that it is to see God face-to-face, as He really is, just as the blessed souls in heaven look upon the Divinity. But the doubtful may object that this is impossible since God is infinite and without bounds but our senses and our capacity to perceive are finite and circumscribed.

To these we reply that it suffices for us now to have this expectation and this promise; although, of course, we do not yet possess fully the means of understanding or explaining it. We shall, in the complete fullness of heaven, behold God with a type of vision which far exceeds our present physical vision. We shall behold the Divinity in its perfect effulgence and its absolute and infinite glory. But the capacity to do this is born of, and reserved for, the transcendent intelligence of the blessed alone. In this lower world where we dwell at the moment, with our fallen intelligence and limited and confused senses, we perceive and experience but random fragments, traces, and shadows of this future bliss.

And we shall behold not only the glory of the most holy humanity of the Son of God but the plentitude of the Godhead which dwells within Him. Indeed, our human eyes would never suffice to sustain this magnificent vision unless strengthened and assisted by the omnipotent Creator of all things. It will be purely by the assistance and gracious gifts of this ineffable Divinity that we shall be made capable of perceiving and comprehending the infinite glory thereof. This shall indeed exceed all that we are presently capable of perceiving, beholding, and comprehending, and therefore may not be meaningfully compared to any earthly joy or temporal happiness, since it will incommensurably surpass it in both extent and nature.

In that ineffable vision, which is ineffable precisely because of the nature of its transcendent object, there will be revealed not only the simple fact of God's existence but each of the perfections which pertain to God. Since God is the Creator, whatever there is of good in created things are present in God—I will not say merely in their highest grade but rather in their utter and complete perfection. This includes power, wisdom, goodness, providence, justice, and mercy. Such divine attributes, according to the infinite scope of their perfection, we shall then perceive fully, not mediated through or reflected by any created thing.

In addition to the perfections of these aspects of goodness whose traces or reflection we experience now in creatures, we shall also behold other attributes which our intellectual capacities are not able, as yet, to comprehend, conceive, or even imagine. These include things which we now experience only through their antithesis in the present world. For example, we often perceive in this world complexity, but we never perceive true simplicity. The unseen attribute of divine simplicity is therefore inferred through an opposition to the complexity which is perceived. Divine immutability is similarly inferred in opposition to the constant mutability which we experience in the here and now. And God's indivisible eternity, while entirely exceeding the capacity of our minds to imagine it, is inferred in contrast to the state of flux and transition which we everywhere behold. Indeed, what is our present existence but an unceasing succession of brief moments, whose coming into existence is virtually indistinguishable from their passing out of existence—instances of time which die as soon as they are born, which cease to be as soon as they are?

God's infinite magnitude, too, is wholly beyond our ability to imagine, yet we may infer it conceptually in opposition to the circumscribed nature and extent of each created thing. And we may infer the perfection of the divine intelligence which, unlike all created intelligences that may only comprehend things separately and in part, apprehends and penetrates all things not only as a collection of individual components but in a unified and instantaneous totality.

And God's perfect, unified, and immutable will and volition may be inferred by contrast to our own wills and those of other people. We experience the human will to be a fluctuating thing, variable from moment to moment, tossed about by passions of love and anger, and swayed by affections and fears. The eternal constancy and order of God's will—which is identical with perfect justice and mercy—though unseen and inconceivable, stands as the antithetical counterpart to that which we currently experience and perceive in all human affairs.

In the kingdom of heaven, all of these attributes of God, which are presented to us now only as contraries to that which we do currently know and comprehend, shall be revealed as they truly are: free from all opposition, imperfection, and limitation, and radiating forth in their purest essence and celestial plenitude.

Furthermore, we shall behold the glorious mystery of the Most Holy Trinity. This shall be in an entirely different mode to how we imagine it at present, which is merely through the shadows of our Faith. This Faith may define in words the doctrine of the Trinity correctly and fairly precisely, and yet it is wholly unable to express or to communicate its supreme and ineffable reality.

But in the kingdom of heaven, we shall fully penetrate the unity of Essence and the Trinity of Persons of the Godhead. We shall comprehend fully how the Father begets the consubstantial

and coeternal Son, and how the Father and the Son together produce one perfect Love, which then becomes the third Person of
the Trinity, the Holy Spirit—of the same divine nature as the
other two.

While we are in this passing world, we are able to speak of
these doctrines only as children reciting formulae, with no real
knowledge or conception of the realities in themselves. But in the
kingdom of heaven, illuminated by the light of divine glory, we
shall fully comprehend the arcane and supernal mysteries of the
Trinity, which is both the generative and impelling cause and the
final object of this sacred and ultimate glory.

Indeed, there will be a great many other mysteries that are
wholly unknown to us in the present world, and which shall be
revealed only in paradise. This multitude of mysteries may not
be the essence of our beatitude—which is the Trinity itself—but
will rather be its manifold effects and manifestations. And these
entirely escape our temporal and earthly nature. Without the
pellucid gleam of supernatural light, these necessarily remain
hidden at present. But with the revelation of such wonders, our
happiness will be entire, not only in its fundamental and deepest essence, but also in every incidental particular and detail.

Among these mysteries will be that of the incarnation of the
Word of God and all that pertains thereto and emanates therefrom—namely, the Resurrection, the Eucharist, the justification
of sinners, and other similar things. All these are truly necessary
to our salvation through the ordination of Divine Providence.
But they shall not be the essential part of our beatitude, which
shall consist in the plenitude of the Divinity alone. Indeed, the
mysteries of our salvation did not come from God as if by necessity or essence, for God would be no less God if such things never
had taken place.

We may trust that there are a thousand other secret and hidden mysteries of eternal Providence which are now wholly unknown to us in this present life. But in the realm of eternity, we shall comprehend them all. By means of these, new and unconceived degrees of blessedness and bliss shall be endlessly bestowed upon us.

In the divine essence of the Godhead, all possible goodness and beatitude shall be inscribed, as if in a compendious or encyclopedic book. We shall perceive and enjoy all the graces, mercies, and consolations which have assisted us in this present life. We shall even enjoy those which we have refused or neglected, due to our current hardness of heart and blindness of spirit.

These good things shall saturate us with the highest degree of joy, and by means of this beatitude, we shall be rendered pleasing to God and similar to God. All past evil actions shall be obliterated and erased. We shall be entirely overcome and suffused with the ineffable goodness of the Divinity. We shall behold clearly all the miraculous blessings of heaven, together with the emptiness of all earthly things. Through perfect contemplation, we shall embrace the essence of the Godhead and be eternally united to God by sublime and chaste love. In such a state, no passing thing or earthly reality will be able to add to or take away from our infinite joy, even in the slightest.

Yet, through our mortal weakness, at the present moment, we remain incapable of comprehending or imagining these things authentically or fully. Yet still, we should be animated by a most fervent desire for all these blessings.

The Sacred Scriptures teach us that what God has prepared for us are things which "eye has not seen, nor ear heard, nor which can be conceived by the mortal heart."[20] Indeed, we deceive ourselves

---

[20] 1 Corinthians 2:9.

by envisaging anything which we are capable of conceiving or expressing. But this very blindness itself ought to be most dear to us because by virtue of it, we are filled with an irresistible and impatient longing for the ineffable and incomprehensible bliss that awaits us in heaven.

For now, we are obliged ardently to love and desire these mysterious and hidden things by the small but certain light of faith alone—yet knowing that, in the eternal life to come, they shall constitute our perfect happiness and our infinite delight. Let us hasten always towards this perfect joy!

Chapter III

On the inferno, and the grievous sufferings and afflictions which abound therein

—————— • ◆ • ——————

I f the immensity and excellence of the good things that are promised to us in the kingdom of heaven are insufficient to move our hearts, the weight, intensity, and interminability of the suffering and torments that await those who have separated themselves from the love of God shall certainly convince anyone. If we are not attracted by the eternal bliss of heaven, shall we not at least fear unending sorrow in hell? Personally, when I reflect upon such things in my mind, my very innards tremble! And this is by contemplating them only insofar as the human mind is capable of understanding and imagining such horrors, not as they really will be.

How greatly will they mourn, all those who find themselves deprived of heaven for the sake of the vain and fugitive pleasures of sin! What bitter regret shall be theirs! One can scarcely imagine what it would feel like to realize that one has sold the infinite riches of eternal joy for the paltry price of some fleeting and sordid sin.

When I consider those who shall end up in such a woeful state, I call to mind the lamentation of Esau when he realized that he had sold his birthright and the paternal blessing of his father Isaac, all for the sake of a mere bowl of lentils.[21] Similarly, I think of that legendary king, Lysimachus of Thrace, who gave up both his crown and his scepter for the sake of a glass of cool water.[22] And not only was he deprived of his kingdom but, out of the sorrow and regret which followed, he lost both his sanity and his life itself. Or I contemplate the sorrow of Jonathan, who was sentenced to death by his own father, King Saul, because he had tasted a single drop of honey from the tip of a stick.[23] Again, I recall the despair of Micah when he found that the idols which he had made for himself with his own hands had been stolen by thieves.[24]

Now, these people lost their birthright, or an earthly kingdom, or their mortal life, or their idols. And they all regretted it most bitterly. How much more must the loss of one's dignity as heir of the supreme and only Divinity be regretted! How much more the loss of a heavenly kingdom is to be lamented than the loss of an earthly one! How much more the loss of eternal life than passing, mortal life! And if the loss of false gods—mere idols fashioned by human skill and imagination—should be the source of sorrow, how much more grave will be the torments arising from the loss of the one true God, the Creator and Redeemer of all things!

---

[21] Genesis 25:29–34; 27:30–36.

[22] Lysimachus of Thrace was an officer of Alexander the Great and had been chosen as his successor. According to Plutarch, when he and his army were afflicted by severe thirst, he surrendered to his enemies in order to obtain a glass of cool water from them.

[23] 1 Samuel 14:43–44.

[24] Judges 18.

Yet there are many people who seem to consider such eternal and spiritual things to be light or trivial matters. Indeed, there are many who, through their actions, actually seem to wish to be deprived of these greatest treasures of all, as if they are intent upon rendering themselves miserable for endless ages.

Just as the folly of such persons is barely comprehensible, so will be their sufferings and regret. Indeed, they will never find any tormentors or torturers who are more cruel to them than they have been to themselves. Within their hearts, conflicting desires rage as in a furious battle. For nature itself, which dictates that every creature should seek the perpetuation of its own being, compels them to desire eternal life. But their sinfulness, which is ever contrary to their true nature, impels them to actions which will lead to their destruction. All souls are bound to love God by a certain necessity in their nature and essence, since God is their Creator and they are fashioned in His divine image. Yet those enmeshed in sin and who despair of the mercy of heaven come to feel an aversion towards God, since they fear Him as a just judge. However, when they seek to rebel against God, they are really taking up arms against themselves. They cannot, by any means, harm the immortal and omnipotent Deity; rather, they simply inflict profitless pain upon themselves.

And for that majority of souls who will need to undergo some form of purification or purgation after the present life, these will be experienced in accordance with the intentions and outlook which they adopt. If they consider that it is the mercy and kindness of God which has granted to them such a process of purification, it shall become sweet and pleasant to them. Drawn forth by the love of God for them and their own love for God, they shall look upon the bliss of heaven and quickly ascend thereto.

But for those who resent the justice of God and refuse to recognize the operation of God's mercy, such sufferings will be intensified and prolonged. Indeed, for those who stubbornly and proudly refuse the love of God, the sweetness of hope will be replaced by the bitterness of despair. If they permit no force of divine love to draw them upwards to the eternal light, they shall inevitably sink but deeper into the abyss of never-ending night and the shoreless chaos of despair. And, at a certain point, such a state will become definitive and impossible ever to change. And, on account of the immortal nature of the soul, even the release of final oblivion will be denied to them.

However Scripture and the venerable fathers may write about such a state, mere words must always fall far short of the reality. Whatever tactile and sensory qualities and sensations we experience in this life—warmth, coolness, and so forth—shall surge forth to an excessive degree, and so thus become veritable torments. Saint Augustine, whose power and purity of intellect is so illustrious and penetrating in all things, accurately identifies the various possible natures of these sufferings, both physical and spiritual. He reduces them to nine principal elements, which are described below.

First, there is a fire which burns, giving forth scalding heat but no light. And the entire ocean would not suffice to extinguish its flame.

Second, there is a chilling cold, as of an artic blizzard. And an enormous mountain of burning fire would not serve to dispel this relentless cold.

Third, there is the cruel and tormenting worm of conscience. This is "the worm which never dies."[25] And, truly, the bite of the worm of conscience exceeds in pain and agonizing mordancy

---

[25]   Mark 9:45.

that of all the serpents and dragons which abide in this earthly valley of tears!

Fourth, there is a most fetid stench, the rank foulness of which is not equaled or approached by anything in this world.

Fifth, there are the whips and rods of the infernal legions of tormenting fiends. These rain down blows with neither cessation nor respite, with indefatigable and unremitting persistency.

Sixth, there is the oppressive density of the gloomy darkness, which is not able to be dissipated or illuminated in any way. This opaque darkness envelopes with blindness all those who enter it.

Seventh, there is the confusion and ignominy with which all the damned will be totally and shamefully suffused. They shall behold the hideous infamy of their guilt and crimes, with all their hidden sins and vices being openly exposed to the view of all. And by no artifice or contrivance shall they be able to conceal the smallest detail of their shameful depravities.

Eighth, there shall be a constant fear and horror arising from the anticipation of the new and unexpected torments which may befall them. They shall hear the pitiable cries of others who are suffering and these shall inspire unrelenting dread, generating a despair unalleviated by the possibility of resignation or acceptance. Indeed, just as the joys and delights of heaven, despite being eternal, are constantly renewed and ever increasing in intensity, so too, the torments of the inferno continue to increase perpetually.

Ninth—and in the final place—there is the grim apprehension of the everlasting nature of such a woeful state to which the damned are forever bound with myriads of unbreakable chains fashioned from black fire and adamantine iron.

Saint Gregory the Great enumerates the torments of hell in a similar way, following the footsteps of Saint Augustine. He also shows them to be commensurate and intrinsically related in their nature to the sins which they serve to punish. For example, those who were ignited by the fires of illicit lust during their earthly life shall be tormented by burning flames in the world to come. Those who were cold in their love towards God and neighbor shall suffer from icy chills. Those who permitted themselves to be consumed by envy shall be bitten by innumerable worms, serpents, and dragons. Those who wallowed in the delicacies and indulgences of the flesh shall be suffocated by disgusting stenches.

Those who were too proud to confess and acknowledge their sins during this mortal life will experience a ceaseless feeling of shame. Those who lived their lives in the darkness of hidden sins and secret crimes shall be surrounded by an oppressive and impenetrable gloom. And those who permitted themselves to be bound by the chains of vice and temptation in this life will find themselves constrained by unbreakable chains in the next world.

Indeed, these torments are so horrendous that we should scarcely dare to credit them, unless Sacred Scripture spoke of them so often and so openly. And just as we are not able to comprehend fully the sublime mysteries of the Holy Trinity nor the joys and delights of heaven, so the full extent of the torments of hell remain beyond our imagining.

Now, there are some who will object that this seems unjust and unmerciful. Why should those who have committed some momentary sin, or even lead their entire life in iniquity—which is, after all, but a moment compared to eternity—be subject to an eternal punishment? This objection is not difficult to answer. It is not merely the duration of the offence which matters but rather its gravity. Since the divine dignity and excellence of God is infinite, to offend against it in any way constitutes a crime of infinite seriousness, gravity, and magnitude.

At this point, I may add the opinions of Saint Gregory and Saint Bernard, which may offer consolation to many. A human being is never eternally condemned, except in the case of those who end their lives in final and unrepented sin, for how a person concludes his life serves as a definitive testimony and witness to the state in which he desires to continue. The ending of mortal life comes to each individual as an opportunity for their final decision and choice, their final determination of will. The mercy of God is indeed infinite and freely available to all. Yet this divine mercy does not annul the ultimate freedom of each soul to choose either misery or bliss, rebellion or love, pain or peace. But once the soul leaves this realm of time and space, its own free choice necessarily becomes eternal and irreversible.

Chapter IV

On the easiness and joy of obtaining eternal salvation, compared with the difficulty and sorrow of incurring damnation

———— ◆ ————

There are those who assert that arriving at the promised joys of paradise involves so much effort and hardship as to be virtually unattainable. It strikes me that such people must be either more foolish, blind, or arrogant than any others. Such people generally also assert, as the correlate of the difficulty of attaining salvation, that the path to perdition is so easy and so filled with pleasures that it is almost impossible for a normal person to avoid.

In the first place, I would ask such people, "Should you give up on eternal salvation just because it seems a little difficult to obtain? And will you hasten to eternal damnation just because the path which leads there seems easier?"

Secondly, I would tell them that there is, on the contrary, much that is easy and even delightful in the path which leads to eternal happiness, but a great many difficulties, anxieties, and sorrows in the way which leads to damnation. The apparent pleasures which come from sin always turn out to be deceptions and procure no true happiness or enjoyment, even in this world. Moreover, they are generally followed by consequences which are far from pleasant. Indeed, even if there are some small and transitory pleasures obtained from certain sins, the consequences and complications associated with them unfailingly serve to negate the joy of these fleeting pleasures.

Hence, in the book of Wisdom, we read it written, in the person of sinners, "We are fatigued in the way of iniquity and perdition, and we tread a road that is difficult."[26] Similarly, the prophet Jeremiah admonishes us, "Know and see that it is an unhappy and bitter thing to have deserted the Lord your God."[27] Again, the holy king David at one point thus mourns, "My sins have fallen upon my head, and like a heavy burden they weigh me down."[28]

The same sentiment is expressed by the illustrious Saint Augustine, who addresses himself to God in the following terms, "You willed it to be, O Lord, and so it is, that every unruly soul becomes it a punishment to itself." And many of the saints have observed that the action of sin inevitably carries with it its own punishment. For this reason, sin never goes unpunished, since it acts as its own most acute and persistent punisher. Indeed, there is no greater and more certain castigator of sin than one's own conscience and the sorrow, regret, and confusion which arises in the soul as a result of some guilty action.

Take, for example, Cain. Immediately after he had murdered his brother, he began to imagine that thousands of thousands of

---

[26]   Wisdom 5:7.

[27]   Jeremiah 2:19.

[28]   Psalm 37:4.

people would be determined to kill him. This was despite the fact that only his father and mother, Adam and Eve, were the only other people actually in existence at that time. But it is written that Cain cried out, "It shall come to pass that anyone who finds me shall slay me!"[29]

In another place, Sacred Scripture, speaking of sinners, describes their situation thus, "The sound of terror is always in their ears. If they find apparent peace, it is always filled with hidden snares. And in whatever direction they look they shall find a sword awaiting them."[30]

Even those who consider things by the light of reason and human experience alone must admit that conscience never permits a guilty person to feel completely secure, even when there is no immediate or obvious danger of punishment or exposure. For those who walk in darkness or who are blind, it is always difficult and laborious to make a journey, even when the path is quite straightforward and safe. For those whose spiritual vision is clouded by the darkness of sin and guilt, the path of life will always be perilous and tortuous, as if it were strewn with thorns and prickles.

Now, someone may well object to this, quoting the Gospel passage which states, "The way which leads to perdition is wide and easy, and trodden by many. But hard and narrow is the way that leads to life, and there are few who find it."[31] In response, I would suggest that the way to perdition is wide only because it is trodden by so many. It is described as being easy because it *appears* to be easy. The path of sin does not openly advertise all the thorns and spines which plague it, and those whose eyes are

---

[29]   Genesis 4:14.

[30]   Job 15:21–22.

[31]   Matthew 7:14.

blinded by vice generally fail to perceive them until it is too late. The path which leads to life is described as being narrow and found by few because it is granted only as a grace of God through faith, and not discovered by purely human efforts. Yet this grace, despite being a precious and wonderful gift, is freely given. And it is described as being "hard" only because it entails hard consequences for those who do not follow it or refuse and resist it.

Of course, we are all called "to carry our crosses"[32] to arrive at eternal beatitude. Yet this carrying of one's personal cross is often accompanied by spiritual blessings and tranquility of soul which more than compensate for it. The weight of bearing the cross which the Gospel prescribes for each disciple of Christ is always less oppressive than the weight of the alternative burden of sin, since it is lightened by divine grace. Moreover, the weight of the yoke of goodness is sweet, whereas the weight of the burden of sin—which is never any less or lighter—is always unspeakably bitter.

Of course, I am not naïvely saying that the road which leads to heaven is continually filled with nothing but roses and delights. Since the Head of our Faith and the Author of our salvation was Himself crowned with thorns, we can scarcely expect to escape suffering entirely.[33] Nevertheless, I maintain that the difficulties and suffering which we encounter along the way that lead to salvation are far less than those encountered by those who follow a path that leads to perdition.

If the plotting and scheming of the wicked do not come to fruition, they are afflicted with disappointment and frustration. But if their schemes *do* come to fruition, they soon experience boredom or satiety with what they have obtained. This experience of

---

[32]   Cf. Matthew 10:38, 16:24; Mark 8:34; Luke 14:27.

[33]   Cf. John 15:20.

boredom or satiety never affects God Himself, of course, and it seldom affects saints and those people who lead a truly virtuous life. Yet for those who indulge in sin and depravity, they are generally soon overcome with boredom, satiety, and even disgust and nausea at what were initially guilty pleasures.

But when individuals who have become entangled in sin and depravity give up these activities to pursue a path of piety and repentance, they are almost always filled with a profound joy and a deep sense of relief.

There is generally nothing more inconvenient and more troublesome to the happy and smooth conduct of life than the vices, especially those vices which spring from lust. As soon as these lusts cease to perpetuate and renew themselves, they become like heavy and tedious burdens. Those who placed their hopes of happiness in the fulfillment of what were initially the most burning and ardent of carnal desires soon find the fire of these desires to fade. And, generally, it is soon entirely extinguished. Their former illusions of possible happiness are then replaced by nothing but disgust, boredom, and misery.

But love and fear of God is quite a different type of motivation from the impulses of lust. Love and fear of God are motivating forces which direct souls steadily and calmly. They do not fade away or grow tiresome but rather increase in solidity, substance, and delight the more assiduously and committedly they are pursued. Those who follow them diligently, as twin flags leading their souls into the bliss of eternity, find sweetness even in suffering. Through faith and purity of conscience, they discover an imperturbable and stable tranquility in the flux of changing and adverse things.

The one who loves God alone comes to fear God alone. Such a person will laugh at all the adversities of this world. But the person who desires or fears the things of this fluctuating world—which are given or taken away by capricious fortune and random chance—shall never find any stable or enduring peace. Even when he comes to possess what he has desired and has escaped that which he feared, his heart will still be subject to anxiety, since mere chance or a random convergence of circumstances could change everything for him at any time.

Could there be anyone who does not realize that it is best to serve the Lord, who, though capable of justified wrath, much prefers to forgive? Could there be anyone who does not realize just how perilous it is to give one's loyalty to this passing and inconstant world—which, sooner or later, casts down all those whom it raises up, and eventually takes away all that it gives?

Sorrow is the unfailing and constant companion of the pleasures of vice. Such pleasures immediately vanish, and their duration is verily but of a moment. But even that moment itself is filled with all manner of torments and anxieties. Yet, on the contrary, the toils and efforts of virtue are filled with a hidden sweetness for all those who keep in mind the anticipation of the eternal beatitude which most surely awaits them.

Jesus Christ declared to be happy all those who suffer persecution for love of him. He promised the kingdom of heaven to such people.[34] Is there anyone who, knowing such a thing, shall not fervently desire to share in the cross? Is there anyone who could be cognizant of the certain reward which God has promised to those who fear Him and the innumerable blessings which shall be poured out upon him, and who shall not then readily submit himself to the will and counsels of this same generous and benign God? Is there anyone who would not open himself to accepting all the treasures of divine joy, simply by abiding in the happy love and fear of God?

---

[34]   Cf. Matthew 5:10.

Those holy martyrs whose lives are described in the book of Maccabees were certainly inspired by such considerations when they boldly spoke the following words to the wicked king who was about to execute them: "You may destroy us in this fleeting earthly life. But the King of the universe shall raise us up in the resurrection of the eternal life, the true life, since we have died out of allegiance to his law!"[35] There is indeed a veritable multitude of holy men and women who have maintained perfect serenity in accepting suffering. By their example, they have shown how much sweetness there may be found in undergoing present deprivations and sorrows for the sake of guaranteed future joys and delights.

The one who loves God finds a certain peace in bearing adversity for the sake of this love. As many theologians have maintained, charity and grace always share the same dwelling place. Therefore, whoever tolerates adversity or deprivation for the sake of the love of God will, in the very act of tolerating such things, receive a gift of grace capable of imbuing him with complete peace and serenity. This grace, being of divine origin and divine in nature, is always more than commensurate with and more lasting than whatever hardships one may be called upon to undergo.

It is commonly said that for the one who loves, nothing is too difficult. There is surely no one who has ever truly loved who has not felt this. Indeed, we come to love even the labors or efforts we make for the sake of pleasing our chosen beloved.

Hence, I believe myself to be justified in concluding that if we truly love God and truly desire eternal happiness, whatever we are called to do or to undergo for the sake of this final happiness shall become sweet and enjoyable. On the other hand, there is no one sufficiently foolish or dull as to love the possibility of his own

---

[35] 2 Maccabees 7:9.

eternal perdition. For this reason, whatever deeds or actions lead to eternal perdition can never truly be sweet and or genuinely enjoyable.

The path which leads to eternal sorrow must itself necessarily be strewn with sorrow. But the path which takes us to eternal delight will, by its very nature, be illuminated and graciously infused by the pleasant anticipation of the joys and sweetness to which it leads.

CHAPTER V

On motivating one's soul towards the pursuit of the eternal joys of heaven

———— ◆ ————

I t is pertinent to note at this point certain indisputable and self-evident truths. Firstly, we are all created by God. Consequently, each one of us is signed by something of the character and image of the Divinity. We were created for no other purpose than that we might enjoy the eternal life of heaven. And we were redeemed at the price of Christ's precious blood so that we might become heirs of His glory.

Secondly, the whole course of this mortal life is nothing more than a brief moment or a mere instant when compared to the boundless infinitude of eternity. But our eternal happiness or eternal unhappiness depends entirely upon this brief and passing moment of earthly life. The delights and eternity of paradise call our souls to seek them out with the greatest and most compelling insistence and diligence. Conversely, the horror and dread of everlasting perdition should more than suffice to motivate us to wish earnestly to escape them. But even without such considerations of the life to come, even in this world the joys and tranquility of living virtuously are manifestly preferable in every respect to the anxiety and misery of living sinfully. As has been shown, the way which leads to perdition is filled with thorns, but the path taking us to heaven is filled with flowers of sweet delight.

All of this makes me wonder how it can be possible to take so much trouble about the things of this present life, as so many do, but to neglect the far more consequential things of eternity. Shall we be occupied with, and discriminating in, those delicacies which pertain merely to the mortal body while remaining insensate and dull to those which pertain to the immortal soul? If we are scarcely able to tolerate many of the small ills and tribulations which befall us in this present life, do we really think that we shall be able to carry the weight of eternal perdition and everlasting torment? If we value so highly those worldly honors, pleasures, and delights which are but illusory—or, at best, momentary—shall we neglect those blessings which are infinite and eternal?

How could such a thing be possible? Is there a single human being who would really choose a life of passing misery to a life of eternal happiness? No one of sound mind could possibly give preference to unending death and suffering than to boundless joy and the plenitude of immortal delight. To do such is to fly in the face not only of faith and the divine law but of reason and nature itself.

If God had created us for the present life only, it would be fitting for us to give no thought to any future things. But if we are created for a future destiny, is it not incumbent upon us to give our best efforts towards securing this future destiny? If we dread and mourn death as the termination of this troubled and short mortal life, should we not all the more fervently yearn for a life that is without sorrow, an eternally blessed life that has no end?

The soil in which our souls now grow is the flesh, with its many desires and disturbances, and the world, with all its distractions and anxieties. This is never our true native land. Hence it is that our existence here is never entirely satisfactory and lasts only a little while. Yet we do our best to provide for the necessities of this life and take careful thought for its contingencies. Should we then neglect the necessities of the life to come, which is infinitely greater both in its duration and its possible happiness or unhappiness? Shall we not carefully plan for the contingencies of all eternity?

When Jesus descended to us, He did so in order that He might bestow upon us the grace of ascending to Him. Hence, it follows that our attentions should be seriously directed to obtaining this fruitful and abundant promised land. Each action is performed rightly if it is directed towards its final end, or towards achieving its ultimate purpose. If the final end of our soul's existence is eternal beatitude in the kingdom of heaven, should we not then pursue this with the utmost diligence?

I would like to believe that anyone who has read the five short chapters presented so far will have considered deeply the seriousness of the eternal destiny of the soul and give his heart up to some meditation on this. This present life is but a passing moment and a pilgrimage rather than a resting place. And like all those engaged in a pilgrimage, it behooves us to have in mind our destination and to direct our steps accordingly.

The path that brings us to eternal life is made sweet by hope and becomes beautiful by the anticipation of the celestial delights to which it leads. Moreover, we are constantly assisted by divine grace and love as we walk such a path. In contrast, the road that leads to perdition is turbulent and sorrowful, not only on account of its destination, but even by its very nature.

Let us then heed the voice of God which gently and lovingly calls us to eternal beatitude. Since it is our very nature to desire happiness, let our greatest desire always be for that immortal happiness which infinitely exceeds all others!

CHAPTER VI

On what constitutes
Christian perfection

I t is not without justification that authorities who have analyzed the perfection of Christian life have typically divided it into three different stages. These three stages of life are steps whereby one may progressively ascend to the heights of Christian perfection.

The first stage is referred to as the "purgative life." This stage is concerned with cleansing the soul from vices and from sins, thereby rendering it open to the graces of God.

The second stage is the "illuminative life." In this stage, one develops a deeper and more perspicacious insight into the mysteries of the Faith. The heart and mind are enlightened by a purer and clearer light, and are thus rendered capable of embracing more completely and more fully the secrets of God. Having disempowered the proclivities of vice and sin in the purgative stage, the soul is now free to adhere more fully to the divine will. With the darkness of sin and the distractions of vice cast aside, the eyes of the heart perceive more clearly the realities of celestial truth.

The third and highest stage is referred to as the "unitive life." In this stage, the soul, now purged of sin and illuminated by divine truth, strives to adhere inseparably to God through perfect love. The soul is completely united to the will of God and so becomes forgetful of the self and of the world. It wishes for nothing other than the fulfillment of the will of God in all things.

Indeed, this union of the soul to the divine will through perfect love constitutes the perfection of Christian life. And this may be demonstrated to all, both the simple and the learned, by the following argument. All Christians recognize that they are created by God solely through the grace and liberality of the Creator. Similarly, there is no one who does not realize that God fashioned His creation for no other purpose than that it might partake in His own infinite goodness. Therefore, all persons of sound mind must agree that there can be nothing better for a human being than to act in accordance with the will of the Creator, since it is by, through, and for this beneficent will alone that they exist.

In this is to be found the true life for which were created, and true happiness also, since happiness springs from living in accordance with our deepest and most authentic nature and purpose. Indeed, the Son of God Himself declared that He had no food other than to do the will of His Father.[36] Neither is there any means whereby a person can become closely united to God than by humble conformity and simple obedience to the divine will. It is for this very reason that Jesus describes those who do the will of the Father as being His brother, sister, and mother.[37]

Since God is utterly perfect and free from all defect or possibility of error, it seems clearer than the sun itself that God's will and decree for human actions constitute the definitive and ultimate norm and best standard of moral perfection. Neither is a person

---

[36]   John 4:34.
[37]   See Matthew 12:50.

able to be counted amongst those who have truly chosen God's love unless he also seeks and strives to conform to God's will in all things.

The three forms of life identified above each have their particular purposes and aims, although they are all part of a journey towards the same ultimate goal—namely, the eternal beatitude of the soul and the glory of God. The first stage, the purgative, is intended to cleanse the soul of all stain of sin and make it pleasing in the sight of its Creator. The second stage, the illuminative, seeks to perceive the mysteries of salvation more deeply and embrace it in love. At this stage, not only are sinful actions eschewed, but the roots of sin—the vices of the soul—are identified and subdued. In the third stage, the unitive, the will is brought into complete conformity with that of God, desiring nothing other than what God wills and disposes.

Each of these three stages is directed towards this final end, which is the union of the human will to the divine will. But such a union cannot be achieved until the first two preparatory stages have been diligently undertaken. Purgation from sinful actions is necessary since such sinful actions are always, and by their very nature, out of harmony with God's will. And illumination in the divine mysteries is also required since without such illumination, it remains impossible to discern or perceive the will of God.

In the purgative life, through the motions of grace, we prepare and correct ourselves by developing a genuine hatred of sin and a heartfelt aversion to the vices. In the illuminative life, we dispose ourselves not merely to refrain from sin but to the active cultivation and habitual exercise of the virtues. By progressive steps, this exercise of the virtues facilitates the imitation of the example of Our Lord Jesus Christ. And in following His footsteps, the rule and standard of moral perfection is to be found.

Thus, the purgative stage of the spiritual life may be likened to cutting down the visible tree of sinful actions. This cutting down the tree, though, remains an incomplete work, since the roots of the plant still remain concealed within the earth. In the illuminative stage, these roots of vice, which are the propensity to sin, are uncovered and eradicated, as far as possible. But there remains a third act—that of planting a new tree, nourishing it, and cultivating it assiduously. This new tree is one that shall transcend the bounds of its earthly origins and verily reach unto the celestial heights! Like the heliotrope or sunflower always striving after the golden light of heaven's sun, so this tree aspires to the radiance of the Divinity. It is held to this Divinity by gentle but unbreakable bonds of love that draw it into an ever closer and more intimate relationship. And the fruit it bears is nothing less than complete union with the will of God!

As a person progresses into greater maturity in the Christian life, he takes care not only in the avoidance of sin but even in the removal of the very seeds of sin and the eradication from the soul of the type of soil in which vice can so readily flourish. But this work is never fully complete as long as we remain in this mortal state; rather, it is an endeavor to be continuously and attentively maintained throughout one's entire life.

Indeed, this present life is a continual battleground for the soul. Idleness is the constant origin of vice. It behooves us to struggle industriously and without relaxation against the tendency to sin. This tendency remains in each of us as a consequence of the ancient transgression of Adam. Sometimes, we are called to fight by boldly stepping out, sometimes by firmly resisting, sometimes by striking so that the vice which would enslave us is thoroughly subdued. We are assaulted not merely by the lusts of the flesh but by the phantoms of vanities and the cunning of demons. One cannot merely passively rest in the peace of Christ during this life but must constantly and actively protect that peace against the incursions of its foes. And these foes exist both in the world which surrounds us and within our own hearts.

Yet we do not undertake this battle unaided or unsupported. The divine grace and mercy constantly assist us, as do the sacraments of the holy Church. And there are two particular instruments which equip us most effectively for our spiritual journey. These are the love of God and the awareness of the presence of God.

The love of God and the sense of the presence of God are the two most powerful motives by which a person can purify his conscience from the stain of sin and raise it up to celestial realities. Through the love of God and the awareness of the divine presence, the mind is led to perceive the marvelous wonders of the Lord and the hidden and glorious mysteries of the Deity. Then, by the action of purest grace, the heart is filled with a compelling desire for God and for the bliss of heaven. By means of love, it is inflamed with a more ardent longing for the highest good. By constant awareness of the presence of God, the avoidance of sin and the cultivation of virtuous actions become natural habits.

It is this love of God and mindfulness of the divine presence that render us diligent in pleasing God and studiously intent upon conforming ourselves, our actions, and our wills to God's will. Nothing else can be found which is so efficacious in producing such results. The love of God and the presence of God arm us powerfully against our spiritual foes and equip and prepare us to overcome them. Moreover, if we cultivate these qualities in our hearts, we thereby become the sharers in the divine goodness and possessors of an ineffable treasure—that is to say, a sure formula for peace and tranquility.

From the love of God, perfect obedience arises. It is obvious that to love anyone and then to act contrary to the will and desires of the beloved would be wholly incongruous. Rather, the lover strives diligently to act in accordance with the will of the beloved, to become one with the beloved in mind and heart. And, similarly, if we are in the presence of some person in authority—a prince, or general, or judge, for example—we will naturally ensure that our behavior is in accordance with their commands or instructions and free from any visible impropriety. If we come to appreciate that all that we do is done in the sight of God and that He perceives not only our actions but gazes into the very depths of our hearts and secrets of our souls, should we not take the utmost care to do that which is pleasing to Him and to refrain from all that displeases Him?

It remains for us now to examine the most effective ways of stirring up the love of God within ourselves and cultivating a constant sense of the divine presence. In finding these, we shall indeed have found the most certain means of discerning the will of God and of conforming ourselves to this will. And it is truly in this that the perfection of Christian life consists.

CHAPTER VII

On stirring up the love of God within one's heart

❖

In order to stir up and nourish the love of God in one's heart, there are five considerations which are most useful and effective. It is most beneficial to commit these considerations to memory and to make a habit of calling them to mind at every possible opportunity.

The first of these considerations is that of the common benefits that the human race has received from the gracious hand of God, its Creator and Redeemer. The second consideration is that of singular benefits and particular graces that one has received as an individual. The third consideration is that of the good things that God has prepared for those who love Him. The fourth is the various ills, afflictions, misfortunes, and miseries that we would not be able to avoid except by the protection and benevolence of God. The fifth consideration is the infinite perfections that subsist in God alone and which merit to be loved above all else simply for their own intrinsic and utter excellence.

Firstly, the common benefits that God has bestowed upon the entire race are such as to merit our deepest appreciation and our sincere love for the giver of such benefits. Without any compulsion, God created humanity, bestowing upon it existence itself and giving it the entire earth as its dwelling place and dominion. We were also granted a nature that was, at least before our own transgression, innocent and blessed. Moreover, this nature was such that it was destined for eternal beatitude. And when the human race had fallen by willful disobedience, God did not wish to destroy it—although He was fully capable of doing so and would have been perfectly justified in such an action. Rather, impelled by pure beneficence, mercy, and love, God wished to redeem us.

And God, having willed this redemption, could have achieved it by His mere act of volition or by uttering a single word. Indeed, this was all that had been necessary for God to create the universe, and He could therefore have recreated it just as easily. Nevertheless, the divine heart so overflowed with love for humanity that God chose the mystery of the incarnation of His own Self. This gratuitous act of self-giving on the part of God for our salvation served to manifest His infinite love towards us and to bind humanity to the Deity by a manifold bond of charity, which could never be broken or severed. And shall we, miserable creatures that we are, withhold our love from God who was so free in bestowing His love upon us?

Furthermore, if we consider the infinite power and greatness of God, it is clear that the very least divine action would suffice to produce any finite result or to produce any effect, including our salvation. Yet this would not suffice to express the immensity of God's love for us. Not only did He undergo the Incarnation whereby the divine essence was united with the lowliness and poverty of our human condition, but He accepted even death. And not just any death, but a death of the most horrendous and shameful kind.

God so desired our love that it behooved Him firstly to display the untold depth of His love for us. Not only did God empty Himself of the highest majesty and the glory of His supreme omnipotence for our sake, but He accepted sufferings the magnitude of which cannot be comprehended, sacrificing His very self as an offering of pure love. And shall we, then, be so cold and inhuman as not to respond to this love by loving God in return?

It is pertinent also to consider the great things which God has prepared for us in heaven. Indeed, the joys of this celestial paradise not only exceed all comparison with any earthly joy but transcend even that which we can conceive or imagine. And we are offered this as a free gift, for nothing any human being—even the greatest saint—could possibly do would ever suffice to earn such an infinite reward.

Indeed, after our sins, humanity deserved punishment, or at least death. Yet, rather than do what strict justice demanded, Our Lord redeemed us by the price of His own precious blood. And not content merely to save us from destruction, God opened to us the heavenly realms of eternal life and joy. Is there anyone whose heart is so stony, whose mind so obdurate as not to recip- rocate at least something of this divine love? Indeed, the small love of which the human heart is capable is but an infinitesimal particle compared to the immensity of the love that God has already bestowed upon us!

If we move from these wonderful benefits and graces which God has poured out upon the human race as a whole, each of us shall also find something in our particular lives for which we owe gratitude and love to the Lord. There are those who have recovered from some illness, and those who have escaped grave peril and death. There are those who, despite being bereft of all human help, have managed to survive persecutions and oppressions. Indeed, there is barely anyone who will not find, if he looks deeply into his heart, at least one thing for which he owes particular gratitude to God. The very fact that we still enjoy life and liberty testifies, in most cases, that the grace of God has served to rescue or preserve each individual from some particular peril or predicament. Thus, it is impossible that a Christian—if he is ready to open his eyes to all that he has received—should not feel bound to God by genuine love and profound gratitude.

It is patently obvious to all who consider the matter that *not* to display love towards God, who has bestowed such a multitude of general and particular benefits, must amount to the most stubborn ingratitude. On the other hand, truly loving God is the greatest and most complete way we can repay God for the benefits He has conferred upon us. And since it is purely out of love and as an expression of love that God has prepared for us all the glories and delights of heaven, should we not feel ashamed not to love God in return? God has prepared these things with no desire of receiving any benefit, except that we should return something to Him of His own endless love for us.

It is also pertinent to note the dreadful fate of those who refuse to love God. Indeed, it is the refusal of the demons to love the Divinity that places them into hell, more so than any particular sinful or wicked actions. If the act of loving God assures our eternal happiness and glory, but the refusal to love God will bring about unending misery, who could possibly not choose to love God?

Aside from this, the basic motivation to love anything or anyone arises from the perception of some form or forms of particular goodness within them. Such particular forms of goodness may include beauty, or strength, or honesty, or intelligence, or aptness for some purpose or other. Yet God is the origin and absolute and infinite perfection of each and every possible form of particular goodness. Reason alone therefore dictates that it behooves us to love the Divinity, as the epitome and essence of all goodness, above all else.

I cannot believe that a mind which earnestly exercises itself in contemplating the mystery of infinite and absolute goodness—which is to say, God—can refrain from being inspired with genuine love towards that goodness and experiencing therefrom a certain degree of blessedness.

There are, perhaps, those who love God merely for the sake of avoiding future punishments. These love God, we might say, to the minimal possible extent. But even that form of love, which arises from the barest observance of the requirements of the law, is sufficient to produce salvation and to save the soul from the punishments which it rightly dreads.

Others love God so that they may be worthy of receiving the rewards due to love. This might be called a "mercenary love," insofar as it seeks a reward other than God Himself. It contains an element of self-love since it seeks the benefit of the one who is loving, not the One loved. Nonetheless, this form of love, since it produces observance of the commandments, shall lead to the reward to which it aspires, which is ultimately that of eternal glory.

There are others who love God out of gratitude as a result of appreciation of the multitude of benefits and blessings bestowed upon them by the divine hand. This form of love is less imperfect than the two previous forms. Yet it still falls short of perfection since it is mixed in its object. God is loved, but on account of God's gifts rather than on account of God's self. Yet, as long as the commandments are observed, this love shall certainly lead the soul to a full and complete enjoyment of the divine gifts whose appreciation animates it. This full and complete enjoyment of the divine gifts is found, of course, in their consummation in the eternal joys of heaven.

There are also those who love God not for fear of punishment, or desire for reward, or for gratitude for benefits received from God. These love God simply for God's own sake, on account of His supreme and absolute goodness. This, indeed, is the most perfect form of love. For apart from God, there is nothing which is truly worthy of love. Persons who are filled with this love will follow the precepts of divine law not out of a dread of incurring punishment or a desire to merit a reward but rather solely out of a wish to do that which is pleasing to God and in accordance with his will. This indeed is the highest and most pure degree of love to which the human heart may ascend.

Of course, there are very few human beings who reach this exalted pinnacle of love during this mortal life. But those who do attain to this degree of love—which is given only by the special grace of God—experience a true foretaste of celestial beatitude while still on earth. Infused with the radiance and glory of divine charity, they anticipate, even now, the eternal joys of heaven!

CHAPTER VIII

On the various ways in which God is present, and how an awareness of this presence of God assists the cultivation of Christian perfection

———— ◆ ————

The presence of God may be considered under two different varieties. The first is a *general* presence, in which God is to be found present in all creation and in every single created thing according to its form and nature. The second is a *special* and particular presence, which is to be encountered in certain human beings according to the gifts of His grace. Each of these two varieties of the presence of God may in turn be divided into three further categories.

God is present in all of His creation through the outpouring of the magnitude of His power, wisdom, virtue, and love. Indeed, it was this power, wisdom, virtue, and love from God which formed creation from nothing at the beginning of time and which continues to sustain it in being. Therefore, creation itself, both as a totality and in all its individual works, is a wonderful and irrefutable manifestation of the active presence of God.

God's presence in the world is like the presence of the soul within a living body. The soul performs its work through the members of the body which it controls; and in the same way, God works through the entire universe, giving it animation and life. God works through the created universe, not only by forming, preserving, and animating it in a general sense, but in His presence and influence, which directs created beings to strive for the good and to work in accordance with their own proper nature and virtue.

God, through His particular and special presence, causes His grace to operate through just and righteous human beings. And God manifests something of His glory through human beings who partake of blessedness, happiness, and sanctity. In both classes of people, He displays the genuine and active presence of His unfailing love. And it is through the active presence of God that Christian souls are directed to act according to the norms of the Gospel, exemplified in the life and precepts of Christ Himself. This presence of God operating through human beings was established in wonderful fashion by the incarnation of Jesus, whereby God's divinity and our humanity were inseparably united.

That God must be everywhere in His essence is readily demonstrated by simple reason alone. For unless God were infinite, He would not be God. And since God is infinite, He must transcend all boundaries or limits, and therefore must completely fill all things with His own unbounded divine magnitude. As Saint Augustine declared, God is everywhere, and in every location, God is fully present, both in His creating, animating, and sustaining power and in His very essence. Speaking to God with passionate love in his *Soliloquy*, Augustine declares, "We ought to behold with wonder Thy immensity and fathomless greatness,

O Lord! For there is no place or thing which fully contains Thee, nor is there any place which excludes Thee."

The erudite Saint Thomas Aquinas also offers an argument of infallible soundness for the action and presence of God, both universally and in each particular thing. He shows that all the operations of the cosmos spring from the direct action and immediate presence of God. If we wish to understand his argument perfectly, we must recognize that, in general, there are two means by which actions may be performed. One of these means is to act directly and immediately. The other is to act indirectly, when something is done by the agency or instrumentality of another, when the person or thing causing the action is not actually present. For example, the sun provides light and heat to places where the sun is not actually present by means of sending forth its rays through space. Fire may burn one's hand even when the hand is not actually in the fire by transmitting heat through the air or some other medium. And kings and monarchs may govern the various regions of their realms by means of local governors and representatives in various locations. Now, this kind of action takes place when the source of the action—the sun, the fire, or the king—is not actually present. It may therefore be considered to be imperfect and springs from the finitude and limitation of the entity in question. But all forms of imperfection, finitude, and limitation are incompatible with the nature and essence of God. Indeed, since God is perfectly present in every location (since God is infinite), it follows that every work of God is a direct and perfect work of His will and power, even when it *appears* to be performed by means of another agency.

Moreover, human beings are not able to gain knowledge of things unless they encounter them by means of the senses, by means of which they may draw knowledge. Therefore, a human being is not able to have direct knowledge of a thing which is absent from him. Additionally, no human being—since we are limited with respect to magnitude and therefore circumscribed with respect to location—can possibly have all things present to him at once, and therefore cannot have true knowledge of all things. Furthermore, human beings cannot even have knowledge or perception of all things that are actually present to them in a single instant, but must discern separate things individually over a period of time.

But for God, it is very different. God does not perceive things by means of the physical senses or according to their outward aspect. Rather, He knows them through His very essence. And, since God is infinite, His essence is present everywhere. And not only does God perceive all things, but He apprehends them all fully, perfectly, and simultaneously, not paying attention now to one thing and then to another.

Human beings see merely the external surfaces of things whilst their inner workings often remain concealed and unknown. For since human knowledge derives entirely from perception, it is only those aspects of a thing which can be perceived that we may ever truly know. The movements of the soul or heart and thoughts of the mind of another are often hidden from our notice since they are not directly perceptible. Thoughts and emotions are not colors which may be seen by the eye, nor sounds which may be heard by the ear, nor odors which may be smelt by the nose. But God perceives fully both the interior and the exterior and penetrates the hidden counsels and movements of the heart and mind. This is because God's essence is omnipresent and diffused throughout all creation and every individual created thing. In a mysterious way, He is the cause, exemplar, and paradigm of our very essence, including every motion of the heart and soul.

Although it is impossible for the human mind to conceive properly the nature and scope of God's immense perspective and all-encompassing vision, we may offer here a helpful illustration drawn from human experience. One may imagine two princes, together with an army of military forces assembled on a great plain. Now, let us imagine that one of these princes is positioned on a high mountain from which he can inspect the entire army with one look and take in its working, formation, and organization in its totality with a single glance. The other prince is situated on the plain itself in the very midst of the army. This second prince cannot possibly see the army in its entirety, nor grasp its magnitude, organization, and formation by means of looking. Rather, he can only see the particular soldiers who are near at hand. If he wishes to inspect different sections or divisions of the forces, he will be obliged to move around. Nevertheless, he will never have a full and simultaneous perception of the whole. In a like manner, God beholds the whole universe it its entirety with a single glance, which embraces all things in perfect completion and with perfect comprehension. But human beings see only the particular things with which they have immediate contact and comprehend even these only partially and imperfectly.

But God's infinite perfection does not consist in perfect and complete perception and understanding only. Rather, all creation and all created things must look towards God as their primary cause, and the primary cause of all things. For, as Saint Paul observes, He is "the same God who works in all things."[38] That is to say, God is the ultimate cause of all causes. It is not only by God's virtue and power that all things are created, but every single action is a result of His determination and will.

---

[38]   1 Corinthians 12:6.

The internal actions of God are utterly perfect and fully commensurate with His divine nature. Yet in His external actions, with respect to created things, God acts in a measure which is commensurate with the nature of created things, sometimes, in His infinite goodness, holding back the immeasurable magnitude of His power.

For example, the work and action of God which is performed through human beings is exhibited in a manner which is conformable to human nature. And human beings are imperfect, limited, and ephemeral creatures. Thus, human actions, though ultimately products of God's supreme will, do not exhibit divine eternity, omnipotence, or perfection. Rather, they are always fleeting, limited, and imperfect, in accordance with our mortal nature. The sound made by the human voice disappears as soon as it is uttered; every human thought arises like a wave on the surface on the ocean, soon to sink away and permit another to take its place.

Yet God is fully able, and indeed often does, raise up human actions to a level that transcends the smallness of our nature. We may see in works of great human virtue certain reflections of God's sublimity, greatness, and beneficence in a manner which exceeds the normal limits of human nature. But God wisely adjusts His influence and actions according to our weakness and limitations. Thus, God both leads us to the works of heavenly grace and freely permits us to be led to the works of common, earthly nature.

The very goodness of God causes Him to move our hearts towards noble, pious, and charitable works. Even if these do not partake of a miraculous character, they are clear evidence of the active presence of God. Such human good works indeed fall far short of the plenitude of divine goodness; yet, on the other hand, they often transcend the smallness, selfishness, and fragility of our mere earthly human nature.

But even when human actions do not exhibit any particular grace or goodness, it is still upon God's power and presence that they all ultimately depend. For God is the very source of being for all created things, and the very force of life itself. Without God, no mortal being could exist and live even for an instant. It is God who confers to each created thing its existence and its capacity to act.

Therefore, it should be obvious to all (except the mind totally clouded by the most perverse blindness) that God is never truly absent from us but always close at hand and always present within our hearts. And our sins and vices are clearly not compatible with God's will or His divine nature. For this reason, we are always able—through the power of God which is present and actively working in us—to refrain from sin and to overcome our vices if we so choose.

Should we be so foolish to do things in the presence of God which we should be ashamed to do in the presence of other mortals? Even if our sins are completely unknown to our fellow human beings, can we possibly believe them to be unknown to God, who is universally present and who perceives all?

Indeed, it is impossible for a person who is truly aware of the intimate presence of God at every moment in his life not to deplore deeply any sins he may commit. Those who earnestly desire the eternal salvation of their souls should cultivate the awareness of the continual presence of God, for there is nothing else which is so salutary and useful in avoiding sin.

I do not mean to suggest, however, that this presence of God should become an anxious preoccupation or obsession. For that can easily give rise to unhealthy scrupulousness and agitated disquietude of soul. It suffices to recall consciously the presence of God several times each day and not to admit into one's mind anything which obscures or annuls the awareness of this presence. It is better to have a sense of God as the continual context and background of one's daily actions rather than to cease from actions in order to reflect exclusively upon God's presence.

Indeed, it is better simply to love God than to examine one's heart and soul constantly to determine if one loves God or not. Except by special and particular graces, it is not possible to have the presence of God continually in mind to the exclusion of all else. Those who endeavor to do so generally move backwards rather than forwards in the spiritual life, for they lose thereby thousands of opportunities for performing good and useful works and come to concentrate more on themselves and the state of their own souls than God Himself.

The awareness of the presence of God is something commended to us by many saints as something which is not merely grasped by the intellect but embraced with the affections. This awareness of the presence of God can be cultivated by various small daily actions of consecration. In this way, mindfulness of God's presence becomes a lasting habit of life.

God created human beings for no other reason than that the human soul could serve as a dwelling place for His Divinity. God assumed human nature in order that, having rendered it receptive and amiable to Himself, He might more freely enter into it. When the human soul refuses entrance to God, God does not force His way in but stands at the door, gently and patiently knocking. Shall we refuse to open the door of our soul to God—who created us, loves us, and died for us upon the cross?

Let us constantly bear in mind how good it shall be to enjoy the infinite glory of God in the eternal life of heaven. We can also enjoy the anticipation of this eternal beatitude even in this present life through hope and grace. If we are conscious of this, shall we not take all care to dispose our actions so that we arrive at this state of blessedness and carefully avoid all acts which may cut us off from such immense blessings? The enjoyment of such unending bliss is, after all, the true destiny and the only real fulfillment of each soul.

I do not believe that there is any human heart so hardened by wickedness that it can fail to be moved by such a consideration. God showed the immensity of His love towards humanity in forming us in His image. The moral precepts which He gives us serve no other purpose than the cultivation and perfection of this image and likeness within our souls. Therefore, let us take God Himself as the exemplar, guide, and ultimate purpose of all our actions.

The words of Scripture and the writings of the holy fathers so clearly indicate God to be the exemplar of the correct mode of living that the truth of this proposition is not able to be ignored. Saint Augustine shows that not only is God Himself the model of right living for human beings but He is the *only* true model. Augustine's reasoning here is very acute and subtle. He says that for someone to be a perfect rule or model for our behavior, he would need to be both visible—so that we could observe and follow him—and infallible—so that we are led according to truth. Now, all human beings and mortal ideas are certainly visible, but also fallible, and therefore cannot form a perfect guide. It is God alone who satisfies the criterion of infallibility.

However, God—purely in His transcendent, celestial essence—although infallible, is invisible. Yet through the Incarnation, this same God, without losing anything of His divine infallibility, assumed the visible form of our humanity. Thus, it is God—as the incarnate hypostasis of the Son, Our Lord Jesus Christ—who alone can serve as a perfect rule and model for human conduct. For apart from Christ, we shall find no one nor anything that is at once both visible and truly infallible.

Human souls which have achieved true sanctity take the Redeemer not only as the example for all their actions but as the very foundation of their entire lives. Thus, they endeavor to serve as faithful instruments of Christ's love in conformity with His will. They are drawn to a pure and pious mode of living and undertake to act in accordance with the example of Christ whenever the opportunity presents itself.

For Jesus is indeed the precious prototype of human perfection that ought always to be before the eyes of our minds. In this sense, Christ indeed becomes "all in all things."[39] As Saint Ambrose writes, it is in vain that any human should seek to acquire virtues except by following in the footsteps of Christ, who teaches us Himself in the Gospel that "I am the way, the truth, and the life."[40] Following Saint Augustine's interpretation of this text, it is as if the Lord is answering three questions posed to Him by the soul. The soul asks, "Which way shall I go to arrive at blessedness?" And Jesus answers, "I am the way that will lead you to blessedness." The soul enquires, "In what should I believe?" And again Jesus answers, "I am the divine Truth in which you may safely believe." Finally, the soul beseeches, "Where shall I find eternal life?" And the Lord replies, "I Myself am the life of endless and perfect joy!"

Whoever studiously applies himself to cultivating an awareness of the presence of God and to bringing this presence to its fruition through the imitation of the example of Christ shall readily obtain God's grace and shall retain it without difficulty. And the reception of this divine grace is certainly the principal and highest objective of our earthly existence, for it is most assuredly the one and only means whereby we shall obtain entrance into the glory of heaven and come to enjoy the true and blessed life which knows no end.

---

[39] Colossians 3:11.
[40] John 14:6.

Chapter IX

On distractions in prayer

———— ◆ ————

Virtue is said to be found in taking the middle course in all things. For extremes of anything—in one direction or another—partake of the character of vices and folly. Accordingly, I suggest that true virtue in prayer is not to be sought by taking it to extremes. Taking the practice of prayer to an extreme or excessive level (in respect to time or intensity) would necessarily result in the negation or neglect of other legitimate duties, which are equally assigned to humankind by Divine Providence. Today, there are some who presumptuously present themselves as illuminated or enlightened souls and who foolishly advocate such excesses.

There is a certain false or fallacious leisure which many seek in prayer in which the soul and mind cease from all activity. In such states, the heart itself ceases from acts of emotion, even that of love. Such artificial states of inert quietism are quite different from the genuine state of repose which God sometimes imparts to holy souls. In these cases, the soul ceases all activities, except for a single one—namely, that of loving God. In this state, the soul does not perform any action but rather simply experiences an outpouring of grace. It receives from God rather than giving or seeking.

Such experiences are, of course, by no means identical to the state of the souls of the blessed in heaven. Rather, God imparts them freely and lovingly but temporarily, as an occasional means of refreshing and encouraging those who seek Him.

But sometimes God withdraws spiritual consolations from a soul entirely for a time so that it experiences no sweetness in prayer. In such cases, one should humbly accept this, even if it means that the activity of prayer feels less like prayer and more like penance. Nevertheless, one must be cautious in continuing too stubbornly or persistently with devotions under such conditions, lest the activity of prayer become purely mechanical and wholly divorced from the contemplation of God.

For those who have been involved in busy and demanding activities, they cannot expect their prayer to be entirely free from distractions. This is not in itself problematic or culpable. It suffices that one does not deliberately place an obstacle to the voice of God or give mental consent to inappropriate or improper distractions. In this regard, the nature of various distractions should be rightly distinguished. Some originate from an act of the will, whereas others arise involuntarily. The first kind depend upon a deliberate decision, whereas the latter do not. Of course, the type of distractions which originate from an act of the will are easily overcome simply by ceasing the motion of the will which caused them to arise. Since they are voluntary acts of the mind, they can readily be stopped by a simple decision to do so.

The other kind of distractions to prayer—the kind which appear *involuntarily*—may be divided into three varieties. The first kind simply divert the mind from its proper focus, yet do not undermine the merits or value of its prayer. These are simple distractions of the senses, such as things one may hear or see while praying (or memories of things heard or seen), which are not bad in themselves. To deal with this kind of distraction, it suffices to acknowledge them humbly and to recognize one's fault. One should then turn one's awareness to the presence of God, asking His assistance to restore attention and concentration.

The second kind of involuntary distractions are thoughts which not only turn one's attention from God but also potentially undermine the virtue and fruitfulness of prayer entirely. These are things such as anger, resentment, envy, bitterness, and hatred. They can all spring up in the mind like sparks which soon flare up into a raging fire. The best remedy for these thoughts is zealously to redirect one's attention to God. The use of short, insistent prayers can be very helpful, such as the line from the psalm, "O God, come to my aid; O Lord, make haste to help me!"[41] In these cases, the mind should actively deny its consent to the distracting thought and firmly resist it. If it cannot succeed in doing this, the distracting thought should be considered to be a cross that one must carry, imploring God for the grace of patience and assistance.

The third type of involuntary distraction is when the mind wanders from one theme or image to another, yet is not distracted from its principal object—namely, God. For example, a person may devote himself to prayer intending to meditate upon the nativity of Our Lord but soon he may find himself instead considering His death upon Calvary. Such "distractions" do not lead away from prayer but rather to another form or focus of prayer. Indeed, the soul engaged in prayer should always be ready to follow freely wherever God may choose to lead it.

Sometimes diversions of this nature bring about such wonderful results that one should be hesitant to condemn them out of hand. For example, once the great Saint Ambrose was delivering

---

[41]   Psalm 69:1.

a homily and wandered far from his intended topic. Nevertheless, his words were manifestly directed by God and inspired by
the Spirit. Amongst his listeners at that time was that illustrious
luminary of the Church, Saint Augustine. And he testifies that he
never heard Ambrose preach more eloquently or beautifully than
he did on that occasion. In the same way, God sometimes diverts
prayer from its intended course to lead it to something better,
and even to something exceeding all of one's original hopes and
expectations. Indeed, sometimes divine illuminations come to
pass in this very way.

My advice to people who experience distractions from their
intended focus of prayer or meditation to another focus is that
they should, at first, endeavor to persevere, lest they succumb to
flippancy, caprice, or simple failure of attention. But if they truly
feel that God is calling them to something else, they should freely
permit themselves to follow their inclination. For it may well be
that the Holy Spirit is leading them to something incomparably
better and more profound than they had previously intended.

CHAPTER X

On aridity in prayer

————— ◆ —————

T he experience of aridity in prayer is what suffering and
tribulations are to Christian life in general. Those who
would always walk on a flowery path or rest only on a bed of
roses shall never gain the blessings of heaven. In the same way,
those who wish always to rejoice in uninterrupted sweetness
in their prayer life will not attain spiritual maturity or become
fully pleasing to God. The path which leads to heaven is never
without its thorns and asperities, yet it is nevertheless more
secure, sure, and safe than any other. Just so, the experience
of times of aridity in prayer is a feature of every sound spiritual life. Jesus Christ Himself bravely took up His cross. He
also experienced many instances of aridity in His prayer. While,
as God, He was all-knowing, as a human being, He knew the
darkness of spiritual desolation and sometimes felt that His
prayers were unheard. Indeed, on the cross, He exclaimed, "My
God, my God, why have You forsaken me?"[42]

The perfection of prayer does not depend upon the consolation or sweetness of the emotional response which the person

---

[42] Matthew 27:46.

praying experiences. Rather, it springs from the fervor with which it is made and the sincerity of its intention of pleasing God. The value of any sacrifice consists in it pleasing the one to whom it is offered, not in gratifying the one who offers it. It can happen that devotions which bring pleasure to the person praying are less pleasing to God than those which may be accompanied by a feeling of aridity.

On certain days, a soul may find itself so weighed down by a sense of anxiety and oppressed by dryness that it can barely raise its thoughts to God. It may doubt the possibility of its own salvation and feel that it is utterly lacking in all the graces. It may feel that it is perishing and unable to exercise any virtues, and so be sluggish and tepid in its devotions.

When such feelings come, the best thing is to offer this spiritual suffering itself as a sacrifice to God and to undertake to endure it patiently for the sake of God's greater glory. Thus, even in the midst of such anxieties, one may experience the secret consolation of making such an offering.

And, even though prayer is the true life of the human soul and the unique means whereby persons can both come to know themselves and to transcend themselves, sometimes to cease from prayer is a more pleasing sacrifice to God than to continue in it. I realize this may seem to be an audacious and startling statement and a paradox. Yet many saints have ceased their regular practice of prayer at times in order to attend to the poor or the sick or to perform some other work of charity or utility. This is, indeed, completely consistent with the example of Christ. For it was His practice to withdraw from human company in order to retire into solitude and pray. Yet He was always ready to relinquish this solitude and to cease His prayers when called upon to teach the crowds or to heal the sick or do some other necessary work.

In the same way, one should be ready to cease from prayer—not lightly, of course, but if genuinely called to do so by God or some compelling and valid motive. Often, this call may be in the form of the need to perform some work of charity or some compelling duty. On other occasions, the call to desist from prayer for a time may be purely spiritual—dryness, fatigue, or excessive restlessness. In such cases, whatever appears to be genuinely the will of God should be humbly followed.

Saint Teresa of Avila, the flower of the Church in our own age, has conveyed to us a beautiful teaching, which she relates she received from the mouth of Christ Himself. She tells us that the basis of all human merit is this: to do, to suffer, and to love. She does not include amongst these imperatives "to enjoy," as those who seek only for the experience of sweetness and consolation in prayer would strive to have it. Ultimately, the highest virtue consists in conformity to the will of God, in whatever form and medium it manifests itself.

A word of caution is useful here. If a person finds himself habitually ceasing from prayer for the purpose of doing other and apparently more useful works, it is not unlikely that he is actually heeding his own inclinations more than the will of God. On the other hand, those who constantly withdraw into solitude for the sake of contemplation may also find that they are simply indulging their own preferences and tastes rather than genuinely seeking God. In all things, true virtue is to be found in moderation, in accordance with one's state of life.

It is pure love of God rather than the length of time spent in prayer or meditation that renders a soul pleasing to God. And the more a soul truly loves God, the less concerned it will be about seeking out its own spiritual consolation.

I may conclude this chapter by saying that the aridity and dryness which many people come to experience in prayer should not be seen merely as an affliction to be borne patiently but rather should be accepted in a spirit of obedience and love of God. By accepting it in this manner, even the deprivation of one's customary consolations and former experiences of spiritual sweetness can, paradoxically, itself become sweet.

CHAPTER XI

Twenty spiritual counsels

COUNSEL 1: SPIRITUAL PRACTICES SHOULD BE WISELY ADAPTED TO ONE'S MODE OF LIFE.

Each person ought to adapt his devotional practices to his own mode of life rather than adapting his mode of life to particular spiritual practices which may not accord with his vocation or status in the world. Different species of trees bear their own particular type of fruit, and one cannot expect to pick fruit that does not accord with the species or variety of the tree. In the same way, spiritual and devotional practices must accord with one's own nature, status, and vocation.

There are certain virtues which befit bishops, certain virtues which befit princes, and certain virtues which befit private individuals. Unless a bishop carefully keeps watch over his flock and nourishes them with sound preaching and good example, he cannot hope to be pleasing to God. And similarly with a prince or leader, unless he rules his subjects, preserves peace and order, and punishes wrongdoers, he has failed to do what God has asked of him.

Religious and clergy who are dedicated to the apostolic or active life have fulfilled their duties if they devote a certain proportion of their time to prayer and contemplation, inspired by the example of monastics and contemplatives. But they err if they endeavor to emulate fully the prayer and devotional practices of monastics and contemplatives to the neglect of their other responsibilities.

Each person has his own particular vocation and should adapt his prayer and devotional practices to that. There are many who fall away by striving to attain or perform that which is alien to, and incongruous with, their state of life.

Counsel 2: The fulfillment of one's legitimate duties and responsibilities should be given primacy above any other works of piety or charity.

It is certain that no one will obtain any benefit or merit from performing works that are incongruous with his position and capacity or conflict with the proper responsibilities and duties of his station in life. Take, for example, a wife who gives away large amounts of money to the poor without her husband's knowledge and permission. Although such an action may appear to be a work of charity, it is not, in fact, truly a good work at all. For without the knowledge and consent of her spouse, it is an illicit action.

In the same way, we may imagine a person who is intent upon performing works of charity and, for this purpose, obtains money by some dishonest or disreputable means. Such "charity" would not really be a good work at all since it amounts to theft and giving away the resources of others. By analogy, a clergyman, religious, or government official who—without permission—irresponsibly disperses resources entrusted to his care and stewardship, even if he does so in the name of charity or generosity, acts improperly. After all, these things belong not to him personally but to the Church or to the state.

COUNSEL 3: NO ACT OF DEVOTION SHOULD BE DONE WHICH IS CONTRARY TO THE DEMANDS OF OBEDIENCE OR DUTY.

Any act of devotion, however holy it may seem, is a fault and sin if it is done contrary to the demands of obedience or proper duty. And there are very many people who fall from virtue and grace on account of their pursuit of apparent piety or charity while disregarding the legitimate and immediate demands of obedience and proper duty.

For example, there are many people who devote themselves to saying innumerable Rosaries and constantly visiting churches while neglecting the due and responsible care of their own household. There are wives who neglect their husbands for the sake of such "devotion" and sons who disobey their fathers to practice works of so-called piety.

No matter how avidly people may recite prayers or undertake fasting, these activities have no merit whatsoever if they cause them to overlook their natural and divinely and humanly ordained duties towards their children, parents, or spouse. And not only will such activities be counted as entirely lacking in merit, they may even be viewed as sins before the wise and omniscient judgment of God.

COUNSEL 4: TRUE DEVOTION OUGHT TO BRING DISCIPLINE AND MODERATION TO THE BODY, SOUL, AND SPIRIT, AND NOTHING SHOULD BE UNDERTAKEN WITHOUT MODERATION.

Authentic devotion ought always to tend towards subduing the passions and caprices of the soul.

If any person decided, in order that he might fully overcome the senses of the body, to fast for an entire week but neglected to address the vice of pride, he has not done anything commendable or useful. The spirit, like the body, can indulge in its pleasures, caprices, perversities, and acts of excess. Temperance and moderation are equally necessary for the spirit and the body. Austerities and strictures are never an end in themselves but only useful as a means of achieving their own proper goal. Above all, they serve the purpose and have the objective of rendering the human spirit humble and submissive to the will of God.

Excessive physical austerity and self-denial generally stirs up and agitates the passions of the blood and the desires of the flesh more than subduing or calming them. There are many who consider themselves to have been greatly elevated because they practice harsh fasting or penitence yet who do not truly progress in any real spiritual or moral sense at all.

COUNSEL 5: THE OVERCOMING OF INTERIOR PRIDE IS MORE IMPORTANT THAN EXTERNAL WORKS OF VIRTUE.

Often people who view themselves as pious and holy and believe that they have overcome all vices and faults have not actually done so in the presence of God. For spiritual perfection consists not merely in *believing* oneself to be perfect, which is a form of pride, but rather, we are called to put off the sense of self entirely and to clothe ourselves instead with the example of Jesus Christ. If a person who is naturally subject to feelings of pride finds himself just as proud at the age of fifty as he was when he was twenty, he has not only not made any progress but rather grown even further away from true virtue.

The overcoming of vices and excessive passions is more pleasing to God than any particular work of virtue. Therefore, the one who wishes to progress in Christian life must diligently apply his efforts to the correction of himself. It is culpable to be aware of a fault within one's character and not to attempt to remedy it. And we should never imagine that a virtue that we may possess can compensate for or balance any particular vice.

Each of us is born with a combination of natural good and bad traits in our character. Because we are often praised for our good traits, we can come to delight in these and cultivate them but neglect the correction of our weaknesses, which remain hidden. However, true virtue consists not simply in acting in accordance with our natural propensities but in using effort and reason to correct and improve ourselves.

Frequently, the exterior actions and demeanor of humility give rise to a secret pride within the heart. Many people who make a show of lowliness come to look down upon others who do not display the outward signs of humility. But true humility is always based upon charity; it causes one to think well of one's neighbor, not to judge or condemn them.

COUNSEL 6: ONE SHOULD PAY MORE ATTENTION TO ONE'S OWN FAULTS THAN TO ONES MERITS, AND ONE SHOULD PAY MORE ATTENTION TO THE MERITS OF OTHERS THAN TO THEIR FAULTS.

A piece of advice which is very useful in leading one towards perfection in Christian life is that whenever we consider ourselves, we should pay more attention to our faults than to our merits, but, conversely, whenever we consider other people, we should pay more attention to their merits than to their faults. Each of us is born with a certain natural tendency to judge ourselves more favorably than others. It is for this very reason that Jesus Christ earnestly counsels us in the Gospel to be extremely cautious about considering ourselves as being holier or more righteous than other people.

It is true that reflection on our own faults does not suffice to remove them, but it does generally help to moderate and control them. In contrast, reflection upon our own merits often leads to pride and presumption. And if we do not recognize the merits of others or refuse to acknowledge them, we become unable to improve ourselves by means of imitating them. On the other hand, if we are excessively attentive to the faults and vices of others, we can easily fall into detraction and even calumny.

I urge all those who seek after true sanctity to believe that sincere humility—which is nothing other than honest knowledge of oneself—is the basis of all Christian virtue. If we are constantly and generously observant of the merits of others and equally attentive to faults in our own thoughts or conduct, we shall surely grow both in love of our neighbor as well as accurate and realistic knowledge of ourselves.

Counsel 7: One should exhibit moderation, gentleness, and mercy towards one's own self.

The process of correcting oneself ought to be conducted always with moderation, gentleness, and the quality of spiritual mercy. Otherwise—to borrow an image used by Saint Francis de Sales, the illustrious bishop of Geneva—one risks becoming like a court official who marches around tumultuously, bellowing to everyone else, "Be silent!" in a thunderous voice. Ironically, such a person's actions contribute more to the destruction of the peace and silence which they demand than to its actual promotion.

Surely, we have all observed people who become irritated by matters which are of comparatively minor importance. The fury of their wrath then becomes a greater issue and problem than the original matter which angered them initially. Let us not be like such people in dealing with and correcting our own faults.

On the contrary, if we recognize and acknowledge our faults and weaknesses, we should react with compassion rather than passion, with gentle repentance rather than rigid severity, with kindly exhortations to do better rather than harsh reprimands. Just as a young tree sends forth deeper roots and becomes more fruitful if it is planted in soft and moist soil rather than in hard, dry, and rocky ground, so the soul will flourish more richly in virtue when it is treated with gentleness, lenience, and love.

COUNSEL 8: THE SPIRITUAL LIFE SHOULD BE UNDERTAKEN WITHOUT HASTE OR IMPATIENCE, BUT STEADILY AND CALMLY.

Those who run the fastest at the beginning are not always those who reach their intended destination with the greatest safety and certainty. Often, such runners will stumble and fall. More often than this, they become fatigued and exhausted, and may give up or come to a halt before reaching the end of their course.

For this reason, it is wisest to pursue the journey which leads to salvation moderately and steadily, but without cessation. In this way, the dangers both of stumbling and of becoming exhausted due to excessive zeal or haste are avoided.

There is nothing more perilous at the beginning of one's spiritual life to take as one's example than the practices and approaches of those who are already considerably advanced. It is necessary to proceed gradually, not omitting the basic and initial steps. The first thing the beginner ought to undertake is the moderating and controlling of vices, and after this, virtues should be carefully cultivated. These simple steps should be undertaken before one aspires to such higher spiritual attainments as overcoming the passions or attaining a state of interior peace, perfect detachment, or mystical ecstasy. It is better and more congruent with true humility and simplicity to aim simply at keeping the divine commandments and teachings of the Church rather than going beyond them.

Those rivers and streams which flow gently, moderately, and consistently are by far the most useful to humanity. In contrast, rivers which flow as rushing torrents or turbulent rapids are apt to cause much devastation and are of little practical benefit to anyone. Of course, no one should deliberately resist making progress in the spiritual life according to whatever divine grace offers them, but true grace will never give rise to an impatient or ambitious zeal for spiritual progress, or rather, *apparent* spiritual progress. Such misdirected zeal is always recognizable, for it manifests itself in results which are harmful and troublesome for the person concerned, and detrimental to the happiness and peace of others. It is always sufficient simply to receive whatever graces and spiritual progress God has granted with gratitude and contentment and to trust entirely in His wisdom and discretion in the matter. For truly, God never demands of us more than He has freely given us.

Counsel 9: Inertia and apathy are also to be carefully avoided.

Although, as has just been noted, it is injudicious to attempt to accelerate one's spiritual progress unduly through immoderate zeal or avidity, still, we should also not be slothful or apathetic in our progress. Human life was given to us precisely for the purpose of living, which is to say, of being active in the fulfillment of our goals and vocation. Not to move forwards is, in fact, to move backwards.

There are those who believe, for example, that simply by *not* harming their neighbor, they have done sufficiently well, but merely to refrain from doing evil towards another is not the same as doing good for them.

This type of "holiness" which consists only in refraining from evil is not only imperfect but can even become harmful. The motive of Christian virtue is charity, and simply refraining from causing injuries falls far short of acting charitably. A person who does not violate any laws or decrees of the state but does no positive or necessary work for the benefit of others does not qualify as a good citizen. In the same way, each of us are called to do whatever good we may within the bounds of reason and our capacities and according to what we are rightly called to do in our station in life and vocation.

COUNSEL 10: WORK AS IF EVERYTHING DEPENDED UPON YOUR OWN EFFORTS, BUT WHEN THE WORK IS COMPLETED, GIVE THANKS TO GOD AS IF EVERYTHING DEPENDED UPON HIS GRACE.

Out of all the various pieces of advice one may receive, there is one which can be regarded as most useful and beneficial in all matters of business. Whenever you need to perform some work or complete some task, apply your efforts to it fully, as if nothing depended upon God but everything depended upon your work. But once the task is brought to a successful completion, thank God as if everything was due to Him, and nothing was due to you.

Counsel 11: Joy is a sign of secure faith.

Sadness and melancholy are poor and unfitting companions to devotion, but joy is a faithful testimony to the truth of one's faith. The apostle Paul tells us that "God loves a cheerful giver,"[43] and David, in the Psalms, invites the just to "exultation in the Lord."[44]

Nonetheless, there are many who fall into the error of believing that they are not truly pious unless their austerity and compunction urges them on to a certain melancholy and severity of demeanor. This type of attitude is contrary to genuine piety. For, by reconciling the human soul to God, true devotion should fill the heart with joy and peace so that it experiences sorrow in nothing, except for consciousness of itself falling into a state of mortal sin.

Counsel 12: Sound devotion should lead to tranquility of heart.

Tranquility of heart should be the companion of true devotion. Excessive and turbulent fervor and the desire to test or exert oneself more than others in piety of self-denial are not things which are ever pleasing to God. Such types of labor often demonstrate a lack of trust in God's grace and assistance, as well as excessive reliance on one's own efforts, and God shall refrain from helping those who rely on themselves rather than Him!

Counsel 13: Sin can very easily become a constricting habit.

The sins which should be most carefully avoided are those which lead to more or greater sins. And those sins and vices

---

[43]   2 Corinthians 9:7.

[44]   Psalm 32:1.

which bind and entangle us in bonds that are hard to break are to be deeply dreaded.

All forms of impurity are perilous and pernicious. But fornication is one hundred times more so than any other. The longer it continues, the stronger and more stubborn become the chains by which it binds, and the harder it becomes to escape.

To continue in any sin is the same as being unrepentant for that sin. For no one who is genuinely repentant for an action continues to perform the same action. The dangers of persisting in immoral deeds are clear, for such sins soon become habits or part of one's accustomed mode of life and ultimately lead to a bad end.

COUNSEL 14: A SINGLE FAULT IS ENOUGH TO UNDERMINE MANY VIRTUES.

It is a common and true adage that a single fault is enough to undo a person. Take, for example, a bishop who is chaste and pure and diligent in giving alms. He may indeed be so good that it seems to people that God Himself is in his debt. Yet, if this bishop neglects a single essential part of his duties, he cannot be accounted as having performed his office well.

Or imagine a married woman of irreproachable modesty and pious character. She may come to believe that she has far exceeded her husband in merit and goodness—which may, in fact, really be the case. Eventually, she no longer pays the respect to her husband that is legitimately due to him, and so permits herself to act in disobedience to him. And thus, despite her many good qualities, she slips into sin and can no longer be counted as being a good wife.

All the virtues are closely connected and dependent upon each other. If one is missing, all the others then suffer. Just as no one can be counted as a good worker who neglects even one part of his duties, so no one can be counted as truly virtuous who neglects the cultivation of even a single one of the virtues.

COUNSEL 15: MORAL PERFECTION IS TO BE FOUND IN ACTIONS, NOT WORDS OR THOUGHTS.

A person should not be regarded as more perfect in Christian virtue simply because he is more learned and wiser in discoursing on the Christian virtues or the doctrines of the Faith. For true moral perfection depends not upon knowledge or discourse but upon actions and conduct.

We attain nearness to God through rectitude of our actions rather than through an abundance of sacred learning alone. God asks from each human being the dedication of his heart to Him, above all things. Thus, the simpleton who offers his entire heart and soul to God—even without knowing anything of doctrine, theology, or moral distinctions—is closer to God than the most learned person who is illuminated with many profound insights yet who does not dedicate himself to God so completely. Indeed, such a person must be accounted even further from God because he should know better what it behooves him to do in relation to his conduct and devotion and yet still fails to do it.

COUNSEL 16: NOVELTY IN THE SPIRITUAL LIFE SHOULD NOT BE SOUGHT FOR ITS OWN SAKE.

In matters of prayer and spirituality, to seek out new ways and methods typically involves departing from the tried and trusted approaches of experience and history. This is generally a perilous and unprofitable endeavor. And yet there are today many who do precisely this. Indeed, novelty always tends to please the senses and to attract attention and curiosity, so there is nothing more characteristic of human nature than to seek out that which is new. And there are many who do not consider themselves to be truly pious unless they have developed some form of innovation of their own in their approach to prayer or spirituality.

Examples of such people, who are intent upon novelty, abound. For example, there are consecrated religious who decide that they are showing singular reverence to the Blessed Sacrament by refraining from receiving it, except very rarely. And this is often done contrary to the proper rule and observance of their own religious order. And there are those who, under the pretext of mystical or particular illuminations, allow themselves to succumb to the opinions of heretics and schismatics. And there are even misguided and foolish souls who, believing they have attained to perfect indifference to all material things, permit themselves to practice the sins of the flesh as if they were of no consequence to their salvation. The less said of such people, the better!

Excessive cleverness in matters of spirituality and novelties in devotion are equally hazardous. One should avoid such things like sharp razors or piercing thorns! People who promote and exploit spiritual novelties often stray far from the true faith in Jesus Christ. They often have the love of God on their lips but only self-love in their hearts. They do not revere God how He wishes to be revered—namely, through the Sacred Scriptures and the doctrines and practices of the holy Catholic Church. Rather, they fashion idols out of their own invention and then venerate these with minds made blind by vanity and delusion.

For the person who believes that God may not be found except through new approaches of his own invention is, in fact, seeking God only through himself, or seeking his own exaltation and aggrandizement under the name of God. And he shall, of course, find thereby nothing but empty vanity and pretension. It is perfectly proper, fitting, and sufficient to seek the Divinity through the conventional and ordinary spiritual and sacramental means given by God through His Church. This is infinitely preferable to being led astray by the caprices of one's own personal preferences and being distracted by vain and unnecessary attempts at innovation.

Those who, through the desire for singularity and novelty, deviate from the teachings and practices of the one true Church separate themselves from Christ's mystical body and the means of salvation He Himself has provided. Surely the Lord will declare to such people, "Depart from me, for I do not know you!"

COUNSEL 17: SPIRITUAL PERSONS NEED TO GUARD THEMSELVES AGAINST HIDDEN PRIDE OVER THEIR OWN VIRTUE OR PIETY.

It is very necessary for persons intent upon progressing in the spiritual life to observe themselves carefully, lest pride should surreptitiously make its way into their souls. A certain type of secret pride often creeps into the hearts of spiritual persons that causes them to judge the actions of others and to assume that they themselves are more virtuous than their fellows. Such persons often come to look upon the world and society which surrounds them with disapproval, which they reveal either in their words, actions, sighs, or general manner.

When I speak of refraining from condemning the actions of others, I am not referring to wicked, malicious, and sinful things which are done through free will; of course, crimes and acts of immorality, evil, and cruelty can never be tolerated or approved. Rather, I am speaking of those things which are done without bad intention yet which may seem somewhat imperfect. In many cases, such things happen due to human weakness or lack of prudence rather than any evil intention. And both love and wisdom demand that what is done without evil intention should not be condemned.

Judgment of the actions of others—except in the necessary cases of deliberate crimes and sins—damages the virtue of humility and harms charity. It leads to presumption in placing oneself above one's peers. To do this is contrary both to human prudence and to the teachings of Christ.

A spiritual person should not consider it permissible to condemn any actions of others except those which are very clearly evil. Nor should he speak words of condemnation against any person or deed unless he is absolutely sure of the facts of the matter and, even then, to speak such words only when to refrain from making a condemnation would be to commit an act of injustice or to imply approval of a crime or sin.

Counsel 18: Those involved in the spiritual guidance of others should not allow themselves to be deceived. Those responsible for making pastoral appointments should not allow their decisions to be swayed by persons of high station.

My personal experiences of the things which often take place in this world urge me to request that religious and clergy, and others who are involved in the spiritual care of souls, observe two particular points very carefully and diligently.

The first is that they do not permit themselves to be easily deceived by the pretext of piety and be led astray by those whose virtue is shown only in their face and words but not in their actions. There are many people who speak all the more powerfully and movingly about their religious feelings the more their own actions become wicked and sinful.

I realize, of course, that it is a great merit for a Christian always to endeavor to think well of one's neighbors. But it is perilous to do so when such simplicity is not tempered by the virtue of prudence. I have heard of, and come to witness, innumerable problems and difficulties arising from excessive credulity and gullibility and know of many things that have taken place which are truly unspeakable. Those who are charged with the care of souls or who hold some public office will surely fall into a multitude of errors unless they join something of the wisdom of this world to their commendable moral goodness.

The second point is one which many religious leaders fall into, who think that anything is permitted when it comes to making appointments, especially when these appointments are influenced by patrons of high standing.[45] This indeed creates many problems. Those who are responsible for making appointments often—under the influence of high-ranking personages—are led to choose candidates for pastoral positions who merely meet the minimal requirements of canon law but are not otherwise suitable. And such people end up being appointed rather than those with more genuine fervor or zeal for the salvation of souls or more talent for fulfilling the office in question.

The type of people appointed under these circumstances often prove inert and apathetic in their role. While they may do nothing bad, they equally typically do nothing particularly good

---

[45] At the time at which Richelieu was writing, many ecclesial entities (parish, monasteries, colleges, etc.) would have been funded or otherwise supported by members of the nobility, who were therefore sometimes understood to have the right to choose (or influence the selection of) clergy appointed to serve in, or lead, these. Richelieu's opposition to this practice reflects the reforms of the Council of Trent.

either. But the persons passed over—that is, those with ardor, zeal, and talent—would certainly have achieved many admirable things had they been appointed.

In the pursuit of Christian perfection, we must consider culpable not only any bad deeds which are committed but also the omission of good deeds that are reasonably possible and consistent with one's vocation. Thus, those who, through dullness or inertia or under the influence of others, fail to work to their potential for doing good and useful things cannot be counted as being guiltless or without fault, even though they may not actually do anything illicit or wrong.

COUNSEL 19: THE DANGER OF
EXCESSIVE OR OBSESSIVE MORAL SCRUPLES.

Scruples[46]—or tendencies towards excessive or obsessive moral caution—are to be avoided as much as sin, for both tend towards the same end. Both, in fact, separate the soul from the grace and goodness of God and the fullness of life that God intended for us.

Sin separates us from grace and so deprives us of true life. Scruples, on the other hand, place an obstacle between the soul and good works and God's blessings, and so, like sin, they prevent a person from experiencing life in its fullness.

Sin is, of course, detestable, for by its very nature, it separates the sinner from God. Scruples are also to be studiously avoided. For, though persons suffering from scruples often sincerely intend to seek God, the effect is to remove the soul from God and to close the heart to receiving His divine gifts.

---

[46] "Scruples" is a term traditionally used to describe excessive or unreasonable concern about moral or devotional matters (e.g., obsessive concerns about complying with rubrics, or overly analytical examination of one's own motives and thoughts).

Just as an excessively timid horse who flees from every shadow and breeze will often end up falling into a ditch, so a scrupulous person, who is terrified of the very shadow of sin, ends up hurling himself into an abyss of confusion and uncertainty.

Inordinate reliance on one's own judgment and inordinate responses to fear are often the source of scruples. Thus, an effective remedy for a person afflicted by scruples is to submit himself and his actions to the judgment of another, specifically an experienced spiritual director. In this case, the scrupulous person does well to imitate the example of one suffering from a physical infirmity. Such people are rarely cured unless they follow the guidance of a physician. In the same way, the person tormented by scruples should follow carefully the instructions of a wise spiritual director and accept his judgments with faith and confidence.

But I say a *wise* spiritual director here advisedly. For just as an unskilled doctor will often aggravate a disease more than curing it, so an inept spiritual director will often promote scruples rather than alleviate them.

Despite the virtual impossibility of relieving a person of obsessive scruples without a skillful spiritual director, there are two pieces of advice which are most helpful in this regard. These are offered below.

The first piece of advice is to hold firmly in one's mind the fact that God descended to this lower world and gave His own blood—which is infinitely more precious than the entire world—for the purpose of saving the souls of humankind. He is not, therefore, going to permit a single soul, which was purchased as so immense a price, to be lost for any little or trivial matter.

To this should be added the realization that though the devil is intent upon harming and destroying humankind, he has no real power whatsoever over any soul which detests him and loves God. His temptations are all in vain, unless a soul should be so perverse as to knowingly, consciously, and deliberately choose to succumb to them. It is not what enters the mind of a human being that has the power to damage the soul but only that which the soul deliberately chooses by the act of its own conscious will. Even though sinful faults may enter the mind, unless the will knowingly embraces these, they do not imperil salvation. And even though one may commit improper actions from time to time, unless they are done with a deliberate intention and full cognizance of their sinfulness, they are to be counted as errors, misjudgments, and manifestations of fragility rather than crimes.

Since a person suffering from scruples has an excessive fear or phobia of sin, it is clear that such a person cannot also *wish* to sin. And since, as has been shown, the involvement of deliberate and conscious volition is a necessary condition for something to be a sin, the scrupulous person may consider himself safe from sinning in whatever matter causes him anxiety.

My second piece of advice is that those prone to scruples should avoid focusing their thoughts on the source of their anxieties. Just as, for a sick person, there is nothing more harmful than constantly to think of one's own sickness, so it is for the person afflicted by scruples. Solitude and self-reflection, which are normally healthful practices, will often simply make things worse for him.

I realize, of course, that it is difficult for a sick person not to think about his own sickness. But I urge all those afflicted by scruples to take my advice and to consider their anxieties as mere phantoms and shadows, and imaginary delusions of no real meaning or consequence. By doing this, they will soon overcome these debilitating thoughts and enjoy the freedom which befits the children of God.[47]

COUNSEL 20: TO ACT ALWAYS OUT OF LOVE FOR GOD IS THE SUREST WAY TO ACHIEVE MORAL PERFECTION.

Any person, regardless of his vocation or state of life, is able to be certain that his own life is pleasing to God, as long as what he does is motivated by a love for God and consistent with divine law. For in the love of God and the observance of divine law, the highest rule of all human life is to be found.

I do not speak here only of those who have made religious vows, for these vows enshrine obligations which are proper to those called to particular states of consecrated life. Those who are vowed to such consecrated life indeed bear much rich and noble fruit. But even people in secular life—in the midst of the business of the world—are able to attain Christian perfection by fulfilling well their state, vocation, duties, and role in society. Indeed, they are able to reach moral and spiritual perfection, in accordance with status and condition, just as much as those in consecrated life.

Just as all human beings are different in their physical capacities and strength, so also people are unequal in the capacities of their souls and hearts. But God asks of us only things which are suited to, and commensurate with, the capacities we have. God assigns to each person duties which are proportionate to his capacities. For to ask of any person things which exceed his strength and ability would be unjust and unreasonable.

Although I have already spoken of this reality often, I can think of no better way of concluding my counsels than by a brief

---

[47]   Cf. Romans 8:21.

recapitulation of it. For this may be considered as the essence and heart of my entire book. Our goal has been to offer a means of attaining perfection in the Christian life. The highest exemplar and model of this perfection is, of course, Jesus Christ Himself.

None is able to exceed the limits of his individual capacities and state of life, yet all are called to progress to the fullest extent they can within these limitations. And there is no surer and effective way of doing this than by sincerely imploring God, through the precious blood of Christ, that He pours forth the grace of His virtue. Through this virtue, all things are made possible and easy!

To this gracious God—Father, Son, and Holy Spirit—be all glory and honor forever and ever. Amen.